The Elements of MATLAB®

The Elements of MATLAB Style is experienced MATLAB programme of standards and guidelines for creating solid that will be easy to understand, enhance, and maintain. It is written both for individuals and for those working in teams where consistency is critical.

This is the only book devoted to MATLAB style and best programming practices, focusing on how MATLAB code can be written in order to maximize its effectiveness. Just as Strunk and White's *The Elements of Style* provides rules for writing in the English language, this book provides conventions for

- Formatting
- Naming
- Documentation
- Programming
- Testing

It also includes recommendations on use of the integrated development environment features that help produce better, more consistent software.

Richard K. Johnson has taught dozens of MATLAB courses for universities, companies, and the federal government. He is the author of *MATLAB Programming Style Guidelines* and the developer of the *Data Visualization Toolbox* for MATLAB. He has a Ph.D. in Engineering Science from University of California, San Diego, and is a former professor at Oregon State University.

The Elements
of
MATLAB® *Style*

Richard K. Johnson
Datatool

CAMBRIDGE
UNIVERSITY PRESS

CAMBRIDGE UNIVERSITY PRESS
Cambridge, New York, Melbourne, Madrid, Cape Town, Singapore,
São Paulo, Delhi, Dubai, Tokyo, Mexico City

Cambridge University Press
32 Avenue of the Americas, New York, NY 10013-2473, USA

www.cambridge.org
Information on this title: www.cambridge.org/9780521732581

MATLAB® is a registered trademark of The MathWorks, Inc.

First published 2011

Printed in the United States of America

A catalog record for this publication is available from the British Library.

Library of Congress Cataloging in Publication data

Johnson, Richard K., 1948–
The elements of MATLAB style / Richard K. Johnson.
   p.   cm.
Includes bibliographical references and index.
ISBN 978-0-521-73258-1 (pbk.)
1. MATLAB.   2. Computer programming.   3. Computer software –
Quality control.   4. Numerical analysis – Data processing.   I. Title.
QA76.73.M296J64   2011
518–dc22   2010034949

ISBN 978-0-521-73258-1 Paperback

Contents

Preface

In 2002, I wrote a brief set of observations and thoughts on MATLAB® style for my coworkers. Other programmers found it useful, so I posted the "MATLAB Programming Style Guidelines" document on my website datatool.com. It has since been downloaded more than 40,000 times.

This book responds to that encouraging interest and incorporates what I have learned in the meantime. It joins a well-received series of style books on other languages, including *The Elements of Java Style*, *The Elements of C++ Style*, and *The Elements of C# Style*.

Much of the advice in this book may be familiar. This is deliberate because many of the programming principles described are valid across programming languages. However, the content has been extensively reworked and expanded here to address the unique characteristics of the MATLAB language and development environment environment, as well as the priorities and practices of MATLAB programmers.

Audience

This is a practical manual for the serious user who wants to become more productive. It provides guidance on clear and effective programming, particularly for those who develop with or for others.

This book is written for new MATLAB programmers who want to develop good habits, as well as for experienced

MATLAB programmers who want to get better and to understand why others use different style conventions.

This book is not intended to teach you the MATLAB language, but rather it focuses on how MATLAB code can be written in order to maximize its effectiveness. It assumes you are already familiar with MATLAB programming.

Introduction

> Style: 1b. the shadow-producing pin of a sundial.
> 2c. the custom or plan followed in spelling,
> capitalization, punctuation, and typographic
> arrangement and display.
> — *Webster's New Collegiate Dictionary*

The syntax of a programming language tells you what code it is possible to write – what machines will understand. Style tells you what you ought to write – what humans reading the code will understand. Code written with a consistent, readable style is robust, maintainable, and contains fewer bugs. Code written with no regard to style contains more bugs, and it may simply be thrown away and replaced rather than supported and extended.

Attending to style is particularly important when developing software as a team. Consistent style facilitates communication because it enables team members to read and understand each other's work more easily. The value of consistent programming style increases dramatically with the number of people working with the code and with the amount of code in the project.

Two style guides are classics: Strunk and White's *The Elements of Style* and Kernighan and Plauger's *The Elements of Programming Style*. These small books work because they are simple: a list of rules, each containing an explanation and examples of correct, and sometimes incorrect, use. This book follows the same pattern.

Some of the advice in this book may seem obvious to you, particularly if you have been writing and reading code for a long time. You may disagree with some of the specific suggestions about formatting, naming, or usage. Some guidelines will require trade-offs, for example, making identifiers meaningful, easy to read, and of modest length. The most important message is that you practice consistency. Departures should be a conscious choice.

What I tried to do here is distill decades of development experience into an easily accessible set of heuristics that encourage consistent coding practice (and hopefully help you avoid some coding traps along the way). The idea is to provide a clear standard to follow so you can spend your time solving the customer problems instead of worrying, or even arguing, about things such as naming conventions and formatting.

Issues of style are becoming increasingly important as the MATLAB language changes and its use becomes more widespread. Usage has grown from small-scale demonstration or prototype code to large and complex production code developed by teams. In the early versions, all variables were double-precision matrices; now many data types are available and useful. Integration with Java is standard, and Java classes can appear in MATLAB code. The MATLAB language now has its own object-oriented features. These changes have made clear code writing more important and more challenging.

The goal of these guidelines is to help you produce code that is more likely to be correct, understandable, sharable, maintainable, and extendable. Here is the test: when people look at your code, will they see what you are doing? The spirit of this book can be pithily expressed as "Avoid write-only code."

Several practices can help you become more productive with these guidelines. Understand the motivation. There will be times when you do not want to follow a guideline. Understanding the motivation will help you decide what to do. Choose the guidelines that work for you. Be consistent. Using some set of guidelines consistently is better than inconsistent practice.

Follow the guidelines *while* writing code. Do not expect to go back and apply them later. They are not just window dressing. They really do help. Make the guidelines part of the code inspection process. Teach them to new programmers. Adopt them incrementally if that works better in your situation.

Disclaimer

I dramatically simplified the code samples used in this book to highlight the concepts related to a particular guideline and to fit the relatively narrow text width of the book. In many cases, these code fragments do not conform to the conventions described elsewhere in this book. Do not treat these fragments as definitive examples of real code!

Some elements of the MATLAB product change from release to release. The guidelines in this book apply to recent releases, but some of the details may apply only to the most recent.

1.

General Principles

Good software gets the immediate job done. But great software, written with a consistent and readable style, is predictable, robust, maintainable, supportable, and extensible. A few general principles provide the foundation for great software.

1. Avoid Causing Confusion

Avoid doing things that would be an unpleasant surprise to other software developers. The interfaces and the behavior exhibited by your software must be predictable and consistent. If they are not, then the documentation must clearly identify and justify any unusual instances of use or behavior.

To minimize the chances that anyone would encounter something surprising in your software, you should emphasize the following characteristics in its design, implementation, packaging, and documentation:

Simplicity   Meet the expectations of your users with simple functions, classes, and methods.

Clarity   Ensure that each variable, function, class, and method has a clear purpose.

Completeness   Provide at least the minimum functionality that any reasonable user would expect to find and use.

Consistency   Design similar entities with a similar look and behavior. Create and apply consistent standards whenever possible.

Robustness Provide predictable, documented behavior in response to errors and exceptions. Do not hide errors, and do not force users to detect errors.

2. Avoid Throw-Away Code

Apply these rules to any code you write, not just code destined for production. All too often, some piece of prototype or experimental code will make its way into a finished product. Even if your code never makes it into production, someone else may still have to read it.

Anyone who must look at your code will appreciate your professionalism and foresight at having applied consistent rules from the start. That person may well be you, looking at the code, trying to figure it out long after you wrote it.

3. Help the Reader

People who read your code are not passive. They actively try to interpret and organize it in their brains. You can help the reader by making your naming consistent with meaning, by using layout consistent with logical organization, and by supplying additional relevant information. You may well be that reader, even while writing the code.

4. Maintain the Style of the Original

When modifying existing software that works, your changes should usually follow the style of the original code. Do not attempt to rewrite the old software just to make it match a new style. Rewriting old code simply to change its style may result in the introduction of costly, yet avoidable defects. The use of different styles within a single source file produces code that is more difficult to read and comprehend.

If the existing style is problematic, then consider changing the style of the entire file to make it consistent. Use of Smart

Indent to clarify structure through layout is relatively safe. Carefully changing the comments for compatibility with the Help browser is also worth considering. If you make changes, then be sure to run regression tests and any existing software that interacts with the module.

5. *Document Style Deviations*

No standard is perfect, and no standard is universally applicable. Sometimes you will find yourself in a situation where you need to deviate from an established standard. If so, then strive for clarity and consistency.

Before you decide to ignore a rule, you should first make sure you understand why the rule exists and what the consequences are if the rule is not applied. If you decide you must violate a rule, then document why you have done so. Some organizations will have reasons to deviate from some of these guidelines, but most organizations will benefit from adopting written style guidelines.

2.

Formatting

Graphic designers have long known that the appropriate use of space around and within text can enhance the reading experience. Use layout, white space, and visual organization to clarify relationships and avoid straining the reader's short-term memory. When you modify your code, preserve layout and spacing to make sure that its format is correct. Code that is easy to scan and read is more likely to be correct.

Layout

The purpose of layout is to help the reader understand the code. It should accurately and consistently represent the logical structure of the code. Indentation is particularly helpful for revealing code structure and patterns to provide context for individual statements.

6. Keep Content Within the First Eighty Columns

Avoid writing code in long lines. Short lines are easier to read than long ones. In general, the readability of text decreases as column width increases. The recommended eighty-column width is a common dimension for editors, terminal emulators, printers, and debuggers.

Readability improves if unintentional line breaks and horizontal scrolling are avoided when passing a file between programmers. Limiting lines to eighty columns also makes side-by-side viewing in two windows easier.

7. *Split Long Code Lines at Graceful Points*

A long line is one that exceeds the suggested eighty-column limit. If you have two or more statements on one line, then write each on a line of its own. If a line is too long because it contains a complicated expression, then rewrite the code to make one or more subexpressions on separate lines. Give the subexpressions meaningful names. Keep parenthetical elements together, if possible. The statement

```
if isnan(thisValue)&(thisValue>=initial
Threshold) &~ismember(value,valueArray)
    :
end
```

should be replaced by something like

```
valueIsPresent = ~isnan(thisValue);
valueIsValid = thisValue >= initialThreshold;
valueIsNew = ~ismember(thisValue, valueArray);
if (valueIsPresent && valueIsValid && valueIsNew)
    :
end
```

If the line is still too long, then wrap it at a point that is most easily readable. In general, break after a comma, right parenthesis, string terminator, or space. For example,

```
thisComment = ['All values above ' ...
    int2str(threshold) ' are discarded.'];
```

If the line is still too long, then wrap after an operator:

```
currentThreshold = baseValue+thisOffset- ...
    thisFudgeFactor;
```

8. *Indent Statement Groups Three or Four Spaces*

Good indentation is probably the single best way to reveal program structure. It can set off groups of statements from other code. It can also clarify the beginning and end of loops or conditional statements.

Indentation of one space is too small to be clearly visible, so indentation of two spaces is sometimes suggested to reduce the number of line breaks required to stay within eighty columns for nested statements. However, two-character indentation is marginally visible, and in any case, MATLAB code is usually not deeply nested.

Indentation larger than four spaces can make nested code difficult to read because it increases the chance that the lines must be split. Indentation of four spaces is the current default in the MATLAB Editor; three was the default in some previous versions.

Do not rely on counting spaces for indentation. Establish your standard in the Editor Preferences menu. Match both the tab size and indent size settings to achieve consistent display.

9. Indent Consistently with the MATLAB Editor

The MATLAB Editor automatically provides indentation that clarifies code structure and is consistent with most recommended practices for C++ and Java. If you use a different editor, then set it and your MATLAB Editor to produce consistent indenting so that you can easily transfer code.

Indentation problems when using the Editor usually occur when the code is not written in sequence, for example, when code is inserted with copy and paste or another case is added after a selection construct is initially written. Use the Smart Indent feature in the Text menu to provide uniform indentation at the right places.

10. Do Not Use Hard Tabs

If you use the MATLAB Editor, then select the option "Tab key inserts spaces" in the Preferences menu. If you use a different editor, then do not rely on hard tabs for indentation.

Hard tabs can easily produce different amounts of indentation when displayed in different editors.

11. Put Only One Executable Statement in a Line of Code

This practice improves readability and allows the JIT/ Accelerator to improve performance. Putting multiple statements on one line for conditional constructs or loops lacks an indentation cue for the reader. It may also produce lines that are too long. One line conditional constructs also tend to leave out the often important `else` code.

Replace the conditional

```
if beta >= delta, alpha = beta; end
```

with

```
if beta >= delta
    alpha = beta;
end
```

Replace the one line loop

```
for k = 1:10, y = k.^2; end;
```

with an indented loop.

```
for k = 1:nValues
    y = k.^2;
end
```

12. Define Each Variable on a Separate Line

Using one line for multiple definitions tends to produce over-crowded expressions, variable names that are too short, and unnecessary literal numbers.

Replace

```
rows=10; cols=5; array=zeros(10,5);
```

with the more readable and more flexible

```
nRows = 10;
nCols = 5;
array = zeros(nRows, nCols);
```

13. Use Argument Alignment if it Enhances Readability

Code alignment can make split expressions easier to read and understand. Aligning the new line with the beginning of the similar expression on the previous line can also help reveal errors. Avoid using hard tabs for this alignment because the alignment may not be maintained in all editors. For example,

```
weightedKids = (boyWeight * nBoys) + ...
               (girlWeight * nGirls);
```

However, this type of alignment can be tedious to establish and maintain. It is not needed to make simple cases readable. The lines

```
foopattern(parameter1, parameter2, ...
           parameter3)
settext(['Long line split' ...
        'into two parts.']);
```

are no clearer than

```
foopattern(parameter1, parameter2,
    parameter3)
settext(['Long line split'; 'into two parts.']);
```

If you have many expressions aligned in a statement, then this is probably a sign that you should rewrite the statement using intermediate variables.

In general, do not align definition statements. Replace

```
x =         3;
y =         4;
diagonal = 5;
```

with

```
x = 3;
y = 4;
diagonal = 5;
```

14. Avoid Heavily Nested Code

Heavily nested code, particularly in `for`, `if`, or `switch` constructs, should be rewritten to avoid unnecessary scrolling of the Editor window. Several practices can be used to reduce the amount of nesting. Straightforward vectorization can sometimes help reduce `for` loop nesting because most MATLAB programmers are used to reading it. In some cases, use of the `switch/case` construct may support less nesting than the use of `if/elseif`. The use of cell arrays with case may be more readable than a string of logical expressions with `elseif`. It may be helpful to extract some of the nested code into a function or subfunction.

White Space

15. Include White Space

Inline white space, the use of blanks or spaces, enhances understanding of the code by making the individual components of statements or expressions stand out. It is a major contributor to readability.

16. Surround =, &, |, &&, and || by Spaces

Using space around the assignment character provides a strong visual cue separating the left- and right-hand sides of a statement.

Replace

```
simpleSum=firstTerm+secondTerm;
```

with

```
simpleSum = firstTerm+secondTerm;
```

Using space around the binary logical operators can clarify complicated expressions. The statement

```
a<b && c<d
```

is easier to visually parse than

```
a<b&&c<d
```

17. Use White Space Around Operators When it Enhances Readability

Putting spaces around all operators is controversial. Some programmers find that it enhances readability. Others prefer shorter lines.

Compare the widely spaced

```
simpleAverage = (firstTerm + second) / nTerms;
scale = 1 : nIterations;
```

with the tight

```
simpleAverage = (firstTerm+second)/nTerms;
scale = 1:nIterations;
```

with the intermediate

```
simpleAverage = (firstTerm+second) / nTerms;
scale = 1:nIterations;
```

Putting white space around all operators is not as common in MATLAB as it is in some other languages because MATLAB is a mathematically oriented language and the custom is to use less horizontal spacing for generic variables with short names. In practice

```
z = x+y;
```

is more common than

```
z = x + y;
```

Also, putting spaces around all operators can obscure any structure within a compound expression.

Replace

```
(a + b * c) / (d * f - g)
```

with

```
(a+b*c) / (d*f-g)
```

18. Follow Commas with a Space When it Enhances Readability

These spaces can make code that includes multiple arguments easier to scan. The line

```
foo(alpha, beta, gamma)
```

is more readable than

```
foo(alpha,beta,gamma)
```

In contrast, when the identifiers are short, the expression can look better without the space.

```
foo(x, y)
foo(x,y)
```

It is common practice not to include spaces after commas that separate array indices. Do not put spaces before a comma, colon, or semicolon.

19. Insert Spaces for Multiple Commands in One Line

Putting multiple statements on one line is not recommended. If you choose to do it, then insert spaces to help the reader distinguish statements from expressions.

Replace

```
if (nElements>1),disp('Yes'),end
```

with

```
if (nElements>1), disp('Yes'), end
```

20. Do Not Put Spaces Just Inside Parentheses

Do not put spaces immediately after a left or before a right parenthesis, bracket, or brace. Use of this extra spacing is tedious to apply consistently and does not enhance readability.

21. Do Not Follow Function Names With a Space

MATLAB allows space between a function name and the left parenthesis before its input arguments. When you avoid inserting this space, it is easier to distinguish the function and command forms. Do follow a keyword with a space so that it does not look like a function.

22. Do Not Space Out Semicolons at the End of Lines

Using a column of semicolons to visually define a block of code is a leftover practice from the days of line printer listings that is no longer needed or desirable. Maintaining the alignment when the code is changed is much more trouble than it is worth.

Code Blocks

23. Break Code of Any Appreciable Length into Blocks

Blocks read like paragraphs and help the reader chunk the code. Each block should be cohesive, performing a task such as initializing variables, checking parameters, or computing a task. The code lines in the block should be fairly self-contained with well-defined information passing to other blocks.

Comments can precede a code block to summarize its purpose and provide any important explanations.

24. Separate Logical Groups of Statements Within a Block by One Blank Line

Enhance readability by introducing vertical white space between logical units within a block. The use of one blank line gives a sufficient visual clue distinct from multiple blank lines between blocks.

25. Separate Major Code Blocks by More Than One Blank Line

You can use two or three blank lines or section markup lines. This allows single blank lines within a long code block while still helping the entire block stand out from the adjacent blocks. The number of blank lines can depend on context. For example, fewer lines are appropriate when followed by a comment for the next code block.

Do not use the comment symbol followed by a repeated character such as * or – to visually define code blocks. This approach might have been helpful when programs were primarily viewed on a line printer listing. It is no longer as important now that comments are displayed in a different color from statements in the Editor. Blank lines establish enough of a break in an Editor window and look better than such ASCII art.

26. Separate Subfunctions by More Than One Blank Line

You can use blank lines or section markup comment lines. This practice allows distinct visual breaks between the main function and subfunctions within a file.

27. Use Editor Cells

Most code will be read in an editor. Use the section markup of Editor cells to provide visual separation between code blocks or subfunctions. In addition to supporting selective execution, cells enhance readability in the Editor and support the Publish feature. A cell break or a cell break after a blank line provides enough visual separation to adequately distinguish code blocks.

Formatting Summary

Format the code to make it more readable. Avoid long lines and multiple statements per line so that the code is easier to scan. Indent consistently to reveal logical structure. Use spaces consistently in appropriate places to make each line easier to read and interpret. In particular, insert spaces around operators and expressions to reveal the structure and meaning of statements.

Write your code in logical blocks that can be read as paragraphs so that the program can be understood in chunks. Use blank lines, comment lines, and Editor cell breaks to make these blocks easy to see. Do not use lines of repeated characters to define blocks of code.

3.

Naming

The purpose of a software naming convention is to help the people who read and write the code understand the program. Understanding the code makes it easier to use, write, or modify correctly. The goal in naming is to use names that are easy to recognize and associate with their meaning and role.

The basic content idea is to use words and character sequences that help connect a name with the entity that it represents. It is a great idea to use names that are intuitive, but developers have surprisingly divergent ideas on which names are intuitive. A more realistic objective is to use names that help the reader understand the code.

The basic visual style idea is to use different visual styles for different identifier types. This makes it easier to recognize the various elements of the language. Clearly, some consistency and differentiation is important. There is a balance in differentiation because having a large number of styles makes for too much to remember. In any case, only a few variations of naming style are available in MATLAB, so the language elements have to be grouped into a smaller number of styles. There is controversy is over how best to do it.

Establishing a naming convention for a group of developers is important, but the process can become ridiculously contentious. There is no naming convention that will please everyone. Following a convention consistently is more important than the details of the convention. Inconsistent practices confuse readers and raise legitimate concerns about code quality.

The choices in this guide are based on the belief that similar elements should look similar, and that common usage in the MATLAB and Java communities should be respected. This section describes a commonly used convention that is familiar to many programmers of MATLAB and other languages.

General

The names of identifiers trigger associations. Good identifier names aid comprehension of both the thing named and the associated code structure. Good names are *very* helpful to both the reader and the programmer. However, coming up with good names is not easy. Keep trying until you get them right. If you change the definition or usage of a variable or function so that its name becomes misleading or wrong, then rename it.

To reduce confusion, identifier names should look dissimilar without intensive inspection. Names should be easy to remember and easy to associate with a meaning. They should also be responsive to their environment (not too short or long). Trade-offs are likely to be required.

28. *Use Meaningful Names*

Use identifier names that convey a meaning consistent with the problem domain or typical interpretation. MATLAB can cope with

```
w = h * n
```

but the reader will find it much easier to follow

```
wage = hourlyRate * nHours
```

Try for descriptive but not overly verbose names.

Replace

```
s, computedYears, numberOfStudents
```

with

```
salary, yearsToRetirement, nStudents
```

Meaningful names make the identifiers easier to understand and remember. Both attributes make the code easier to read, write, and use.

29. Use Familiar Names

If your domain convention is to use "client," do not use "customer" or "consumer" as a variable name. Put the elements of compound names in familiar order. Replace

```
lengthArm
```

with

```
armLength
```

If the software is targeted for a knowledge domain or a user group, then use names consistent with standard practice in that domain or by that group.

Replace

```
imageRegionForAnalysis
```

with

```
roi or regionOfInterest
```

30. Use Consistent Names

Simplify the reader's life by not mixing similar names such as

```
customer, customerData, customerInfo
```

for the same or related values. Organize the data so that it makes sense to use one name or multiple distinctive names.

Similarly, avoid mixing similar action terms such as

```
fetchaccount, retreivestore, returncustomer,
getinventory
```

for the same general functionality.

31. Avoid Excessively Long Names

Names that are too long can be difficult to scan and use. Long names are particularly problematic in visually parsing expressions. Because very long names decrease the readability of expressions and statements, the best names are those just long enough to be descriptive. In general, names longer than fifteen characters are not recommended.

Replace

```
applyThresholdToDataArray
```

with

```
applyThreshold
```

The goal in choosing names is not necessarily to give everything complete and proper names, but rather to give them comprehensible and trackable names.

32. Avoid Cryptic Abbreviations

Make identifiers easy to read by avoiding unnecessary abbreviation or shortening. The use of abbreviations usually makes names less pronounceable and more difficult to remember. Programmers are used to some shortening in compound words, but do not overdo it.

Using whole words reduces ambiguity and helps make the code self-documenting. Because they are often not unique, abbreviations are prone to interpretation and typing errors.

Use

```
computeArrivalTime
```

Avoid

```
comparr
```

In this case, it is unclear whether the intent is compute or compare.

Common MATLAB usage justifies some abbreviations such as col for column, dim for dimension, and h for handle. Domain-specific abbreviations are also acceptable. For example,

```
shuttle for spaceShuttle
tech for technical
meds for medications
```

Some abbreviations might benefit from a defining comment near their first appearance.

33. Treat Familiar Acronyms as Words

Domain-specific phrases that are more naturally known through acronyms should be used as acronyms rather than compound words. For example,

```
html, cpu, cm
```

Use the same convention for capitalizing acronyms as for words.

Use

```
htmlVersion, pdfParser
```

not

```
HTMLVersion, PDFParser
```

or

```
hTMLVersion, pDFParser
```

34. Avoid Names that Differ Only by Capitalization

Names that differ only by capitalization are easy to confuse, and this is an almost certain way to introduce defects. Consistent capitalization is one of the hallmarks of good style.

Do not use FlightTime or Flighttime in the same module in which you use flightTime.

Do not use x and X in the same module. Authors of books and papers sometimes use names such as x and X together for related but distinct entities. Programmers work in a different is context because most readers find it easier to differentiate similar names on the printed page than in code displayed on an editor screen.

35. Avoid Names that Differ Only by One Letter

Choose identifier names that will not be confused. Names within a file should differ enough to be readily distinguished. Names that are almost the same make the code difficult to scan. They also increase the likelihood of unintentional use.

Code written by novices often includes names like a1, a2, a3 or a, aa, aaa. This is usually evidence that the names are not meaningful. Even names that carry some meaning can be problematic if they only differ by one number or letter. The following published code has an error in the third line that is disguised by poor variable naming:

```
total = price * qty;
   total2 = total - discount;
   total2 = total * (1 + taxRate);
```

The intent was

```
subtotal = price * quantity;
discountedTotal = subtotal - discount;
billableTotal = discountedTotal * (1 + taxRate);
```

36. Avoid Names with Hard-to-Read Character Sequences

Avoid names containing sequences such as 111 or 00 because they can be difficult to recognize or spell consistently. Also avoid using lowercase 1 or uppercase 0 as a single-letter name.

37. Make Names Pronounceable When You Can

Names that are pronounceable are easier to read and remember. The audio cues can make names easier to hold in short-term memory. Pronounceable names improve communication with other programmers and also reduce the likelihood of typographic errors.

38. Write Names in English

The MATLAB product is written in English, and English is the preferred language for international development.

Variables and Parameters

Variable names should be easily remembered by the programmer and have a suggestive value for readers; that is, they should help us recognize the meanings of the variables. They should also be consistent with the names of similar variables.

39. Avoid Ambiguous or Vague Names

A good name distinguishes one variable from another. A variable name that has to be deciphered should be changed. Names such as `temp1` and `vec` convey little meaning. If used, they should be limited to very small scope.

Be selective in the use of numbers at the ends of names. The appearance of numbers at the ends of variable names often indicates poor naming. Replace

```
length1, length2
```

with

```
lengthStrut, lengthSpring
```

or better

```
strutLength, springLength
```

There is at least one good use for numbers at the ends of names. They are appropriate for coefficients of equations:

```
a1*x + a2*x.^2
```

40. Name According to Meaning, Not Type

The type or class of a variable is available in the Workspace browser. Including type or class in a variable name creates a headache if the type or class is changed.

Use

```
Customer, step
```

not

```
customer_structure, int_step
```

41. Use Lowercase for Simple Variable Names

This is common practice in the C++, Java, and Windows development communities. For example, use

```
linearity, delta
```

Very short variable names can be in uppercase if they are uppercase in conventional usage and if they are unlikely to become parts of compound variable names. Examples include V and R in electrical engineering and Q in signal processing.

42. Use lowerCamelCase for Compound Variable Names

The lowerCamelCase style starts each word in a compound name with an uppercase letter, except the first word. The use of capital letters makes it easier to recognize the individual words in the variable name. This is common practice in the C++, Java, and Windows development communities. Starting variable names with uppercase is usually reserved for objects, types, or structures in other languages. Use

```
credibleThreat, qualityOfLife
```

Some programmers prefer to use underscore to separate parts of a compound variable name. This practice is common in Unix. Although readable, this usage is generally unexpected and not common for variable names in other languages. Another issue with using underscore in variable names used in graph titles, labels, and legends is that the Tex interpreter in MATLAB will read underscore as a switch to subscript, so you will need to apply the parameter/value pair `'interpreter'`, `'none'` for each text string.

43. Use Meaningful Names for Variables with a Large Scope

In practice, most variables should have meaningful names. A descriptive or meaningful name is especially important when a variable is used in code locations that are far apart. This usage eases the reader's burden of remembering what quantity a variable name represents. Names that are too short are a common problem that obscures meaning; that is, it is easier to understand and remember the meaning of `salary` than `s`.

44. Limit Use of Very Short Names to Variables with a Small Scope

The use of short names should be reserved for conditions in which they clarify the structure of the statements or are consistent with intended generality. In a general-purpose function, it may be appropriate to use short generic variable names such as `x`, `y`, `z`, and `t`.

Scratch variables used for temporary storage or indices can have short names because they do not need to be remembered outside local scope. Variable names in different local scopes also do not need to be unique. A programmer reading such a variable's name should be able to assume that its value is not used outside a few lines of nearby code.

45. Be Consistent With i and j

The letters i and j have long been used as both imaginary numbers and indices or loop counters. There is an inherent conflict in usage with no solution that will delight everyone.

Many code examples in MATLAB and other languages use i and j as a loop counters. Those who favor this usage can establish a different variable for imaginary numbers, such as I, J, or jay, or use an expression of the form 1i, which The MathWorks recommends for speed and robustness.

Those who favor saving i or j for the imaginary number can use different loop counter variable names such as iSample or I. Avoid using both j and J in the same scope because they look similar and thus can be easily confused.

46. Use the Prefix n for Variables Representing the Number of Entities

This notation is taken from mathematics, where it is an established convention for indicating the number of items. Use

nFiles, nSegments

rather than

numFiles, NumberOfSegments

A common MATLAB-specific variation, based on common matrix notation, is the use of m rather than n as a prefix for number of rows, as in mRows.

47. Follow a Consistent Convention on Pluralization

Avoid having two variables with names differing only by a final letter. Be especially careful to avoid unintended mixing of the singular and plural names. Some programmers make all variable names either singular or plural, but others find that this can be awkward. The recommended practice is to use a prefix like this for the singular variable, together with a plural suffix for collections or arrays. For example, the singular thisPoint with the plural points, as in

```
thisPoint = points(iPoint,:);
```

A less common usage for the plural is to append a suffix such as Array. For example, the singular point with the plural pointArray, as in

```
point = pointArray(iPoint,:);
```

48. Use the Prefix this for the Current Variable

When referring to a single member of a collection, use this rather than the:

```
thisPage = pages(iPage);
```

49. Use the Suffix No or Prefix i for Variables Representing a Single Entity Number

The No notation is taken from mathematics, where it is an established convention for indicating an entity number.

Replace

```
tableNumber, employeeNumber
```

with

```
tableNo, employeeNo
```

The i prefix effectively makes the variable a named iterator, which is convenient for indexing. Use

```
iTable, iEmployee
```

as in

```
thisEmployee = employees(iEmployee);
```

Other suffixes that some programmers use are Nbr and Num. The most important consideration in this guideline is to distinguish clearly between a single entity number and the number of entities.

50. Prefix Iterator Variables with i, j, k, etc.

The notation is taken from mathematics, where it is an established convention for indicating iterators:

```
for iFile = 1:nFiles
    :
end
```

Many examples of for loops use the variable name i as a loop index. This practice may be suboptimal, particularly if the loop is long, because it misses an opportunity to reinforce the meaning of the loop index.

For nested loops, the iterator variables should usually be in alphabetical order. Alternatively, some mathematically oriented programmers use a variable name starting with i for rows and j for columns, independent of their position in nested loops.

Especially for nested loops, suggestive iterator variable names are helpful:

```
for iFile = 1:nFiles
    for jPosition = 1:nPositions
        :
    end
    :
end
```

51. Embed is, has, etc., in Boolean Variable Names

Use lowerCamelCase and avoid using the word is as a prefix.

Replace variable names that start with is

`isavalidrange, isMissingData`

with

`rangeIsValid, dataIsMissing`

In some cases, other words are clearer:

`borrowerCanQualify, lenderHasMoney`

This convention avoids confusion with or shadowing of Boolean function names, which usually start with `is` in MATLAB software.

52. *Avoid Negated Boolean Variable Names*

A problem arises when such a name is used in conjunction with the logical negation operator because this usage results in a double negative. It is not immediately apparent what is meant by names such as

`~barIsNotFound`

Replace

`barIsNotFound = true;`

with

`barIsFound = false;`

so that you can use

`~barIsFound`

53. *Use the Expected Logical Names and Values*

A true or valid condition is usually associated with a positive integer or a logical true; a false or invalid condition is usually associated with zero or a logical false. To avoid violating expectations, replace the misleading and error-prone usage

`valid = 0;`

with

```
valid = true;
```

MATLAB associates any nonzero number, even a negative one, with a true condition. It is generally poor practice to rely on this somewhat confusing behavior.

54. Avoid Using a Keyword or Special Value Name for a Variable Name

Reserved words have special meaning and can only be used in specific ways. MATLAB can produce cryptic error messages or strange results if any of its reserved words or built-in special values are redefined. M-Lint will usually catch an attempt to redefine a keyword, but not if this is done inside an `eval` statement. Reserved words are listed by the command `iskeyword`. Special values are listed in the MATLAB release documentation.

Also avoid using a variable name that differs from a keyword or special value only by capitalization or a single letter. The code may work, but it can be difficult to read.

55. Avoid Hungarian Notation

A Hungarian variable name typically involves one or two prefixes, a name root, and a qualifier suffix. These names can be ugly, particularly when they are strings of contractions or abbreviations. A bigger problem occurs if a prefix, as is sometimes suggested, encodes data type. If the type needs to be changed, then all incidences of the variable name need to be changed.

Use

```
thetaDegrees
```

Avoid

```
uint8thetaDegrees
```

Because the Workspace browser lists type, Hungarian notation no longer adds value.

A related MATLAB-specific practice is the use of vec as a prefix or suffix. This practice can be problematic if use of the variable changes to include, for example, two-dimensional arrays.

56. Avoid Variable Names that Shadow Functions

There are several names of functions in the MATLAB product that seem to be tempting to use as variable names. Such usage in scripts will shadow the functions and can lead to errors. Using a variable and a function with the same name inside a function will probably cause an error.

Some standard function names that have appeared in code examples as variables are

```
alpha, angle, axes, axis, balance, beta, contrast,
gamma, image, info, input, length, line, mode,
power, rank, run, start, text, type
```

Using a well-known function name as a variable name also reduces readability. If you want to use a standard function name such as length in a variable name, then you can add a qualifier, such as a units suffix, or a noun or adjective prefix:

```
lengthCm, armLength, thisLength
```

57. Avoid Reusing a Variable for Different Contents

When a variable is reused, its purpose is unlikely to be clear from its name. Reusing a temporary variable in multiple places for different contents can make reworking the code difficult. Reuse variables only if memory is a constraint. If you change the meaning of a variable, then also change its name.

Similarly, avoid giving two interpretations to a single variable, such as a hidden meaning as well as a normal meaning. It would be poor practice to use the variable `pageCount` for a page count, except when it is negative, indicating that it is an error flag.

58. Consider a Unit Suffix for Names of Dimensioned Quantities

Using a single set of units for a project is an attractive idea that is often not implemented completely. Adding unit suffixes helps avoid the almost inevitable unintended mixed-unit expressions or unintended computed results. Do not use an ambiguous single-letter suffix. Replace

`angleR, angleD`

with

`angleRadians, angleDegrees`

If you do not use a unit suffix, then consider including the units in a comment to reduce possible confusion.

Constants

The MATLAB language does not have true constants (at least outside objects). We use naming conventions to provide a visual cue that a variable is being treated as a constant. The main goal in this case is to try to avoid unintentional redefinition of the constant. The best naming and usage practices can depend on the scope of the constant.

59. Use All Uppercase for Constant Names with Local Scope

Constants specific to a single m-file are usually defined in the code and written in uppercase. If the constant has a compound name, then use an underscore as a separator. This is common practice in the C++ and Java development communities, when the constant is only used within a file:

```
MAX_ITERATIONS, CODE_RED
```

Never use sequential underscore characters because they are too difficult to read correctly.

Lowercase names can be used in domain-specific applications if the most common representation of the constant is in lowercase. For example, you can use c for the speed of light or h for the Planck constant.

60. Use Function Names for Constants Defined by Functions

Universal or natural constants such as pi are often defined by a function in MATLAB and written in lowercase. Each constant is the output of a function with the same name as the constant. This practice makes it easy to avoid most of the problems with global constants. It is also graceful in expressions.

```
2*pi
```

61. Use Meaningful Names for Constants

As with variable names, the goal is to make it easier for the reader to remember what the name means. Name constants based on significance, not value.

Replace

```
TEN = 10;
```

with

```
MAX_ITERATIONS = 10;
```

Very short constant names can be used if they are conventional usage and unlikely to be confusing to a reader. An example is E for Young's modulus.

62. Define Related Constants Based on the Relation

Defining related constants independently can lead to inconvenient problems with precision.

Replace

```
TWO_PI = 6.283185
```

with

```
TWO_PI = 2*pi;
```

63. Consider Using a Category Prefix

You can prefix the names of constants with their common category. This gives additional information on which constants belong together and what concept the constants represent:

```
CODE_RED, CODE_GREEN, CODE_BLUE
```

Structures and Cell Arrays

64. Use UpperCamelCase for Structure Names

The UpperCamelCase style starts each word in a compound name with an uppercase letter, including the first word. The use of capital letters makes it easier to recognize the individual words in the variable name. This usage is consistent with Java and C++ practice, and it helps distinguish between structures and other arrays:

```
Setup.comment = 'This is a test.';
```

65. Do Not Include the Name of the Structure in a Fieldname

The name of the structure is implicit. Repetition is superfluous in use.

Replace

```
Segment.segmentWidth
```

or

```
Segment.widthSegment
```

with

```
Segment.width
```

66. Use Fieldnames that Follow the Naming Convention for Variables

Structures are convenient for passing variables into and out of functions. Using fieldnames that are the same as variable names enhances readability and reduces the likelihood of typos:

```
Data.unit = unit;
function Result = convert(Data)
      unit = Data.unit;
        :
end
```

is easier to write correctly than using a capitalized fieldname:

```
Data.Unit = unit;
function Result = convert(Data)
      unit = Data.Unit;
        :
end
```

Using fieldnames that are the same as variable names also enables automated packing and unpacking of the structures.

67. Name Cell Arrays Following the Style for Variables

The names of cell arrays should follow the convention for simple variables and arrays. Remember that the goal of different naming styles is to help the reader understand the code.

Because cell arrays use numbered cells, they are more similar to arrays than structures:

```
greetings{1} = 'hello';
```

Functions

Functions are one of the most important and widespread components of MATLAB code. Making their names easy to scan and understand is critical to readability. Try to use function names that succinctly convey what the functions do and suggest how to use them.

A good function name abstracts the details of the function in a way that enhances the readability of a calling function's code without being misleading or confusing. The selection of a useful name depends on what the function does and what (if anything) it returns.

68. Give Functions Meaningful Names

The purpose of a well-named function or method can often be determined just from its name. There is an unfortunate MATLAB tradition of using function names so short that they are cryptic, possibly due to the former DOS eight-character limit for filenames. This concern is no longer relevant and the tradition should usually be avoided to improve readability.

Replace

```
compwid
```

with

```
computehalfwidth
```

or

```
computeHalfWidth
```

An exception is the use of abbreviations or acronyms widely used in mathematics or in the problem domain:

```
max, gcd
```

Functions with such shortened names should have the complete words in header comments for clarity and to support Help browser searches.

69. Name Functions for What They Do

Functions usually perform an action. Naming the function after this action increases readability, making it clear what the function should (and possibly should not) do. Also, this usage can make it easier to keep the code clean of unintended side effects. Typically, function names should start with a verb:

```
plot, reviseforecast
```

You can also name functions for their output. This practice is appropriate if the name would otherwise begin with a common computing verb such as `compute` or `find`. Naming a mathematical or statistical function for its output is common practice in MATLAB code:

```
mean, standarderror, localmaxima
```

70. Follow a Case Convention for Function Names

Using lowercase for function names is standard practice by The MathWorks and most MATLAB authors. It works well for single-word names and reasonably well for short compound names. This practice also helps distinguish function names from lowerCamelCase variable names or UpperCamelCase object names. Using all lowercase also avoids potential filename problems in mixed operating system environments:

```
removebias, adjustbins
```

Using lowerCamelCase for compound function names is the usual practice in other modern languages. It is also becoming more common in code written by The MathWorks and some MATLAB authors. This practice is especially popular for functions that are class methods. Function names often begin with a verb, which helps distinguish them from variable names. For longer compound names, lowerCamelCase is more readable than all lowercase:

`removeVaryingBias, adjustHistogramBins`

These are the preferred conventions, and their use can be mixed.

Two other function name practices are sometimes used. Some programmers use UpperCamelCase. This usage is nonstandard and can cause confusion with class and object naming. A few programmers use underscores in compound function names. This practice is nonstandard. Because it is unexpected, it can actually be more difficult to scan than lowerCamelCase. The underscores are also invisible in the hyperlinks used in reference pages and `help` output. These two practices should not be used, and, in particular, they should not be mixed with the preferred conventions.

71. Reserve the Prefixes `get`/`set` for Accessing an Object Property

This is the general practice in code written by The Math-Works and common practice in C++ and Java development. An occasional exception is the use of `set` for logical set operations:

`getobject, setappdata`

72. Use Expected Verbs in Expected Ways

Consistent use of verbs enhances readability and gives the reader an immediate clue about the task of the function. Consider using `compute` when something is calculated:

`computespreads`

The use of `comp` as a prefix should be avoided because it can be confused with compare. Consider using the word `find` for a search or lookup operation. Consistent use of the term enhances readability and it is a good substitute for the overused and possibly misleading prefix get:

```
findOldestRecord,  findTallestMan
```

Consider the prefix `initialize` when a variable is established. Avoid the abbreviation `init` because it could represent either initialize or initial:

```
initializeState
```

73. Use the Prefix is for Boolean Functions

This is common practice in MATLAB code as well as in C++ and Java. Replace

```
checkforoverpriced
completion
```

with

```
isoverpriced
iscomplete
```

There are a few alternatives to the `is` prefix that fit better in some situations. These include the `has` or `can` prefixes:

```
haslicense
canevaluate
```

A Boolean function can be visually distinguished from a Boolean variable in that the `is` term is a prefix for functions, but it is embedded for variables. Many Boolean functions are available in the MATLAB product. To avoid shadowing them, search the documentation for `is*`.

Avoid using the word `status` in a Boolean function name because it can easily be ambiguous.

Replace

```
licensestatus
```

with

```
haslicense
```

74. Use Complement Prefixes in Compound Names for Complement Operations

Reduce readability challenges by taking advantage of symmetry. Use prefixes such as

```
get/set, add/subtract, create/destroy, start/stop,
insert/delete, increment/decrement, begin/end,
open/close, show/hide, suspend/resume
```

75. Be Selective in the Use of Numbers at the Ends of Names

Do not use a number at the end of a function name to indicate revision. This would require continual modification of calling function code with each function name revision. Such usage would also raise the issue for the reader of whether older versions are of value. Avoid

```
foo1, foo2, foo3
```

Limit numbers at the end of function names to current functions that have different arguments, especially when the functions work for differing dimensionality. For example,

```
interp, interp2, interp3
```

76. Use Numbers Inside Function Names Only for Common Conventions

It is common practice to use the numeral 2 in place of to. The use of other numbers is unusual:

```
str2mat, struct2cell
```

It can be a better practice to replace functions that would use this naming convention with functions that take advantage of polymorphism. For example,

```
daily2monthly, yearly2monthly
```

might be better as a single function

```
tomonthly
```

77. Avoid Unintentional Shadowing

In general, function names should be unique. Shadowing (having two or more functions with the same name) increases the possibility of unexpected behavior or error. Some of these shadowing names that have unfortunately been used in MATLAB code examples are

```
angle, contrast, length, power, rank, type
```

Names can be checked for shadowing using the commands which -all, or exist.

If you do choose to use an existing function name for your function, then put it in a private folder so that execution will not depend on the order of folders in the MATLAB path.

Classes

The use of MATLAB and Java objects is becoming more common in MATLAB code. Follow the Java style conventions for objects and functions to provide consistency and ease of recognition. See *The Elements of Java Style* for additional specific guidelines.

78. Use Nouns When Naming Classes

Classes define objects or things. Use nouns, adjectives with nouns, or noun phrases for their names. Avoid using verbs. For example,

```
Customer, Company, StockMarket
```

79. Use UpperCamelCase for MATLAB Class and Object Names

This usage is consistent with Java practice and with recent usage by The MathWorks. For example, use the class name

```
AccountManager
```

with the object instantiation

```
Robert = AccountManager( ...);
```

80. Use UpperCamelCase for Exception Names

Exceptions are classes, so use the same naming convention. If the exception is an error, then you may choose to append the suffix `Error`. This usage is consistent with Java practice and with recent usage by The MathWorks:

```
try
        :
catch KeyError
        :
end
```

81. Name Properties Like Structure Fields

Use class property names that follow the guidelines for structure fieldnames and variable names. In particular, use meaningful names written in lowerCamelCase. Do not repeat the class name in the property name.

Replace generic names such as

```
Picture.prop1
```

with meaningful names such as

```
Picture.contrast
```

Use lowerCamelCase for compound property names. Replace

`Customer.LastOrder` or `Customer.last_order`

with

`Customer.lastOrder`

Do not include the class name in the property name. Replace the redundant property name

`Picture.PictureContrast`

with

`Picture.contrast`

82. *Name Methods Like Functions*

Most methods are implemented as functions and should follow the same conventions for capitalization. A common practice is to use lowercase for short method names and lowerCamelCase for longer method names. The constructor method is a special case that uses UpperCamelCase because it must have the same name as its class.

Methods perform actions and should be named with action words:

`Amplitude.normalize`

Avoid redundant method names. The class name is implicit and does not need to be repeated. Replace

`Result.updateresult`

with

`Result.update`

83. *Name Accessor Methods after their Properties*

Getters are methods that return the value of a property. You should name a getter method by prefixing the word get to the name of the property, unless it is Boolean. In that case, you prefix `is` to the name of the field instead of `get`:

```
getStamp, isValid
```

Setters are methods that modify the values of a property. You should name a setter method by prefixing the word `set` to the name of the property, regardless of its type:

```
setStamp, setComment
```

84. Use a Single Lowercase Word as the Root Name of a Package

The qualified portion of a package name should consist of a single word that captures the purpose and utility of the package. You can also use a meaningful abbreviation that is common in the project domain.

Data Files and Directories

85. Use Directory and Filenames that are Easy to Work with

Avoid embedded spaces in compound directory and filenames because they can cause difficulties or require special handling in some operating systems. Instead, use the underscore character or hyphen.

86. Use Sortable Numbering in Data Filenames

Data file and directory names often have a meaningful order, either by sequence or date. The MATLAB `dir` function and Current Folder window sort filenames in character order, which may not always be the best. For example, `data11.mat` would be displayed before `data2.mat`.

A simple way around this behavior is to add a large base number so that

```
data2.mat
```

becomes

```
data102.mat
```

and

```
data11.mat
```

becomes

```
data111.mat
```

This format is easily generated in a MATLAB for loop with index iFile as

```
base = 100;
for iFile = 1:nFiles
      fileNo = base+iFile;
      filename = ['data' int2str(fileNo) '.mat'];
      :
end
```

Another technique is to include leading zeros as needed so that

```
data2.mat
```

becomes

```
data02.mat
```

This approach requires a little more work to generate:

```
filename = ['data' ...
sprintf('%02.0f', iFile) '.mat'];
```

87. Use ISO Date Format

It is less ambiguous than other date formats because the fields
are in an internationally recognized order, with a standard
for embedded punctuation. ISO 8601 format sorts well; for
example, 2007-01-31 comes before 2007-02-01. The embedded hyphen (-) is an allowed character in filenames.

Other date formats often use month names that vary with
language and do not sort well. The slash character (/) used in
some other formats is not legal in a file or directory name.

Replace

```
dataJan121999.mat or data12Jan1999.mat
```

with

```
data1999-01-12.mat or data_1999-01-12.mat
```

These ISO filenames can be easily generated in a loop for file
access:

```
mainPart = 'data';
year = 1999;
month = 1;
day = [1:5];
formatSpec = 29;
for iDay = 1:length(day)
     dateNo = datenum([year month day(iDay)]);
     datePart = datestr(dateNo, formatSpec);
     filename = [mainPart datePart '.mat'];
end
```

If needed, a month name can be interpreted or produced using
the month numbers to index into a cell array:

```
monthNames = {'JAN', 'FEB', 'MAR', 'APR', 'MAY',
'JUN', 'JUL', 'AUG', 'SEP', 'OCT', 'NOV', 'DEC'}
```

Naming Summary

Enhance readability by using meaningful, consistent names. Make names easy to recognize and distinguish so that you are likely to use and type them correctly. Avoid names that are vague, misleading, too similar, or difficult to read.

Use capitalization to suggest the role of identifiers such as variables, functions, or classes. Follow the conventions that are common and successful in MATLAB and other languages. Use similar capitalization for similar entities such as functions and methods or variables and properties.

Append prefixes and suffixes if they clarify the meaning or use of a name. Follow common software usages. Avoid prefixes and suffixes that are likely to be distracting or cause maintenance issues.

Avoid name collisions, especially when your variable or function names would shadow existing functions. Use constant names and definitions that discourage unintentional redefinition.

Use variable names that mean what they say. Include standard prefixes and suffixes when they help communicate the role of the variable. Use lowerCamelCase for variable names.

Name functions for the action they perform or the output they produce. Use standard prefixes such as `is` or `get` in expected ways. Do not include temporary or ill-defined version numbering in function names.

Use nouns for the names of classes and objects. Write them in UpperCamelCase.

4.

Documentation

General

There are large variations in the amount and character of documentation for software development projects. MATLAB-specific style issues are concentrated in the internal documentation intimately associated with the code files, particularly comments and reference pages. Documentation of a software routine should clarify what it is doing, as well as define the required and optional inputs and the available outputs. Helpful documentation is aimed at a knowledgeable but not necessarily expert reader who is new to this program, yet familiar with the MATLAB language.

Where possible, the documentation should be generated from the m-file with little effort. The document should have readability features that make it easier to read than simple unformatted comments. In the case of the MATLAB product, this means using the Publish feature.

88. Provide Well-Written Code

The best documentation for a program is clean code. Comments cannot justify poorly written code, nor can they make up for code lacking appropriate name choices, good layout, or an explicit logical structure. Such code should be rewritten.

89. Document Each Module Before or During Its Implementation

Development projects are rarely completed on schedule. If documentation is left for last, then it will get cut short. Such documentation is often too little, too late, or even absent. Writing some documentation early assures that it gets done, and this practice will probably reduce development time. Writing at least some of the documentation before coding will also encourage you to think more about the functionality and interfaces of the modules.

90. Document the Interface for Those Who Will Use It

Clearly describe function usage, input and output arguments, and constraints. Provide the user with enough information to correctly and effectively use the function or class.

91. Document the Design and Implementation for Those Who Will Maintain It

Good code gets used. Code has a life after you write it, and most good programs are not write-once. It is not unusual that good code is modified to increase its functionality or generality. The code modifier will need to read and understand the code. Clear code is essential, but good documentation can be a significant help. With a well-written, well-documented program, making changes is not a painful process.

92. Consider Documenting Some Changes in Header Comments

The best practice is to put any change information in your version control system. Even when you do use version control, checking in many files at a time may lead to inadequate descriptions in the change log. Putting specific information in the comments of each file can make changes easier to track.

If you do not use version control, then changes should be documented in the file. It is usually better to do this in the header comments rather than clutter the code with interspersed comments. This change information is aimed at a maintainer rather than a user. It should be formatted so that it does not clutter the help text or reference page.

93. *Generate HTML Reference Pages*

Provide documentation pages for your code in HTML. Formatted HTML pages are usually more readable than plain text comments. Writing to HTML supports the best compatibility with differing environments for viewing documentation.

94. *Integrate the Reference Pages with the Help Browser*

Integration with the Help browser combines your reference and documentation pages with those included in the MATLAB product. This integration supports use of the same Search, Contents, and Link features that are familiar to MATLAB users. The Help browser and the related Function Browser are the best tools for users to determine the available functionality, the names of the desired functions, and how to use them.

95. *Consider Providing PDF Documentation*

The use of PDF supports bundling the reference pages into a single file for better portability. Reading documentation in a single file can be easier than following hyperlinks through HTML pages. Printing a single PDF file is often more convenient than a collection of HTML files.

Comments

Comments allow programmers to communicate their thoughts in addition to the code. They should add information to the code, not simply replicate it. Typical uses for comments are to explain usage, express the purpose of the code, provide reference information, justify decisions, describe limitations, and mention needed improvements. Well-formatted comments make it easy to generate user documentation using Editor features such as Publish.

Comments close to the code they describe are more likely to be correct and more likely to help code understanding.

Embedding a description in the code file makes it less likely that the code and documentation will diverge, as can easily occur with a separate document. Experience indicates that it is better to write comments at the same time as the code rather than to intend to add comments later.

96. Make Comments Useful

Comments are about communication and nothing else. Comments are guides to the code. Their quality is more important than their quantity. Content-free or ineffective comments are not neutral; rather, they actually make the reader's task more difficult. A bad, irrelevant, or useless comment gets in the way of the reader and is worse than no comment.

Do not comment the obvious. Avoid comments that just restate the code and do not add to understanding. The code itself should make clear what it does. Write comments to describe why or how the code works. Comments addressing why are especially important for code that implements business logic or is domain-specific.

Replace

```
c = zscore(r);   % Apply zscore.
```

with

```
% Center and scale the data.
normalizedRadius = zscore(radius);
```

97. Be Sure that Comments Agree with the Code

Take care that the comment is consistent with the code. Make the action described in the comment consistent with what the code does. Use the same spelling and capitalization for any identifier names in the comments and the code.

The combination of inconsistent comments and poor variable names is particularly pernicious. In this example written by a user, the code performs a count – the test is just a step in the counting. Also, it is counting even numbers, not odd. So, the comment is inconsistent in two ways:

```
% Test for odd numbers.
if mod(x,2) == 0
      oddno = oddno+1;
end
```

To count odd numbers, the code and comment should be something like

```
% Count odd numbers.
if mod(x,2) == 1
      nOdd = nOdd+1;
end
```

If the algorithm behind the original code was the desired action, then it could be rewritten as

```
% Count even numbers.
if mod(x,2) == 0
      nEven = nEven+1;
end
```

Comments referring to edge conditions are especially subject to becoming incorrect when code changes. Delete the incorrect and unnecessary comment:

```
% a must be greater than b
relationIsCorrect = a>=b;
```

98. Revise Comments to be Correct When the Code is Changed

Keep comments current. Comments tend to rot. Avoid this by keeping comments accurate and consistent with the code. When you change the code, change the comment.

The lines

```
% Compute the median absolute deviation.
spread = mean(abs(deviation));
```

probably resulted when the definition of spread was changed in the code but not in the comments.

99. Put Restrictions in the Code, Not the Comments

When you write any comment, consider whether it can be expressed in the code. This is especially true when the comment states any restriction on the actions or variables used in the code. Be alert to the use of "must" or "always" in comments.

Replace

```
% beta must be greater than 0
```

with

```
assert (beta>0, 'Keep beta greater than zero.')
```

or similar code.

If an imperative statement seems to be required in a comment, then be sure that the code implements it.

Replace

```
% Make b between a and c
```

with

```
b = max(b,a);
b = min(b,c);
```

This code is also more explicit about the meaning of "between."

100. Clean up Commented Out Code before Release

The use of version control greatly reduces the need for commenting out code. Sometimes it can be convenient during development, but commented out code should not be released. Just delete it. Otherwise, any future reader would wonder why it was important to leave in the commented out code, which would slow down understanding.

101. Make Comments Easy to Read

As in code, consistency in comment format helps the reader. Readability in comments is more important than proper grammar. Place one space between the % comment symbol and the comment text to support publishing to letter-spaced text. Use two spaces to produce monospaced text. Place comments above and aligned with the code to which they refer.

102. Write Comments for the Publish Feature

The Publish feature of the Editor provides formatted documentation for functions with or without code display, and for scripts with or without execution results. The basic comment format for publishing can be defined with a limited but useful set of special markup characters. HTML is also available for comment markup, but it will, of course, require longer comment text that is more difficult to read in the Editor.

Published comments are usually more readable than unformatted comments because they include features such as headers, bullet lists, and letter spaced and monospaced text. The presentation of the published output will vary, depending on whether you publish to HTML, Word, or some other format.

103. Minimize Use of End-Line Comments

The descriptiveness of end-line comments is constrained by the typical line length, tending to make them cryptic. In general, they should only be used as an adjunct to variable declaration or to identify loop end statements. Other types of comment should usually be on their own line. Very short comments can appear on the same line as the code they describe, but should be spaced far enough apart to separate them from the statements.

104. Consider End-of-Loop Comments

In long nested loop constructs, it can be difficult to visually discern which end goes with which loop. This can be important when there are executable statements between the end lines.

Use a comment after the end keyword that indicates which block is ending. This practice is most useful when an included block is more than twenty lines long or there are more than two levels of nesting. For example,

```
for iFile = 1:nFiles
  for jPosition = 1:nPositions
    :
  end % of position loop
  :
end % of file loop
```

105. Consider Documenting Important Variables Near the Start of the File

It is standard practice in other languages to document variables where they are declared. Because the MATLAB language does not use variable declarations, this information can be provided at initialization or in stand-alone comments:

```
frame = nan(480, 640);  % Size for NTSC.
% points  Points are in rows.
```

106. Consider Documenting Constant Assignments Where They are Defined

This gives additional information on rationale, usage, or constraints:

```
THRESHOLD = 10; % Maximum noise level.
```

107. Use Voice and Person Appropriately

In general, use active voice with second or third person, particularly when the comment refers to nearby code:

```
% Revise currentSpeed based on several fields.
```

and

```
% currentSpeed limits altitudeGoal.
```

Use passive voice and third person when it reads better, which often occurs when referring to state or more distant code:

```
% These data points are normalized.
```

In general, limit the use of first person to temporary comments such as TODO.

108. Use Present Tense to Describe Code

The use of present tense in comments is more conventional and less ambiguous than the use of future tense.

Replace

```
% y will be constrained by x.
```

with

```
% x constrains y.
```

109. Use Complete Sentences in Descriptive Blocks

The text in comment blocks is easier to read when it is in complete sentences:

```
% This calculation uses the Blinkenstaff equation
% as modified by Hershey. The usual variable names
% have been modified to agree with our style.
```

110. You Can Use Incomplete Sentences in One-Liners

Because a one-line comment is adjacent to the code, its meaning can be clear without using a complete sentence:

```
% lower limit on spoonSize.
```

111. Use Short Words

Write comments using short, familiar words. The reader should not need to consult a dictionary to understand the words in a comment.

112. Eliminate Cute Comments

The reader will be justifiably annoyed by comments such as

```
% Do the thing.
% Magic occurs here.
```

113. Minimize the Use of ASCII Art

Do not enclose comments in large boxes drawn with asterisks or other characters. This is an old-fashioned practice and rarely helps readability. These boxes cause visual separation of the comments from the code, and it takes too much time to maintain a consistent look when the text changes. Blank lines before block comments should be enough.

114. Write All Comments in English

In an international environment, English is the preferred language.

Header Comments

The header comments comprise the first contiguous block of comments in a file. A header comment block serves as a preface or introduction. It should contain the purpose of the file and descriptions of the interface (input and output variables). The header comments are usually displayed in the

Help browser or in response to the `help` command without displaying the code, so make them adequate for the user.

Header comments are an exception to the small file rule. They should be sufficient for a new user to use the function properly, as well as a complete quick reference to options and arguments for the sophisticated user.

115. Format the Header Comments for Easy Publishing as Documentation

The MATLAB Publish feature is an excellent tool for automated documentation. Use comment syntax and Editor cell features that support publishing in a clear, easy-to-read format. Include links to figures and equations if they will help the reader understand the purpose or function of the software.

The published output should be consistent with the reference pages for MATLAB standard functions. It should include the function name as a title, a one-sentence summary, input and output syntax, description of what the function does and of its arguments, a list of related functions, and one or more examples. Use the Help Report to list any missing sections in the header comments.

Header comments that are formatted for publishing will also work well when displayed with the help command. Well-formatted header comments look something like

```
%% pho
% Make savory soup.
%% Syntax
%# lunch = pho(meat);
%# lunch = pho(meat, condiment);
%% Description
% pho is a meal alternative to teriyaki.
% The input ingredients are combined with a
% soup base.
```

```
%
% * meat      - a string: 'chicken' or 'beef'
% * condiment - a string: 'cilantro' or 'sprouts'
% * lunch     - a structure with each ingredient
%
%% Example
%# lunch = pho('beef', 'cilantro')
%% See also
% wrap
```

These comments publish as

pho

Make savory soup.

Contents

Syntax
Description
Example
See also

Syntax

```
lunch = pho(meat);
lunch = pho(meat, condiment);
```

Description

pho is a meal alternative to teriyaki. The input ingredients
  are combined with a soup base.
• meat – a string: 'chicken' or 'beef'
• condiment – a string: 'cilantro' or 'sprouts'
• lunch – a structure with each ingredient

Example

```
lunch = pho('beef', 'cilantro')
```

See also

wrap

The Publish feature automatically generates a contents list. This is generally unnecessary in a function reference page, and you may want to delete it.

116. Put the Header Comments in the Right Place

Traditional MATLAB header comments follow the `function` statement. With the new Publish feature, you will achieve better documentation by placing the header comments in the proper format above the `function` statement.

117. Use Title Markup for the Function Name

Put the function name on the first line of the file. Make appropriate use of a `%%` comment line to have it publish as a title. Write a one-sentence summary on the next comment line. This sentence is particularly important when the function's purpose is not clear from its name:

```
%% pho
% Make savory soup.
%%
```

These comments publish as

pho
Make savory soup.

118. Document the Function Interface in the Syntax Section

The user will need to know the input and output arguments and their sequences. The syntax and description sections should provide full enough interface information that it is not necessary to maintain an independent document for this purpose.

The syntax options should start with the most basic options, and then detail the rest of the calling forms. When default values exist, indicate them in the description comments. Use monospaced code format to provide one statement per line:

```
%% Syntax
%# lunch = pho(meat);
%# lunch = pho(meat, condiment);
```

publishes as

Syntax

```
lunch = pho(meat);
lunch = pho(meat, condiment);
```

119. Use the Actual Function Name Case in Comments

Do not use uppercase in the comments when the function name is lowercase. Using uppercase in the comments can cause some confusion because the function name and filename are usually in lowercase. Also, mixed case is beginning to appear in function names, raising the possibility of even more confusion.

The MATLAB product practice is mixed. In the m-file header comments, the function name is often written in all uppercase, which is intended to make the function name prominent when displayed in the Command Window. In the Help browser page, the actual case for the function name is used in the syntax block and description.

Most of us will choose not to maintain independent files for m-file comments and reference pages, so use the actual case of the function name in the header comments.

Replace

```
% PHO is a meal
```

with

```
% pho is a meal
```

120. Describe the Function Arguments in the Description Section

Describe what the function does and how to use it well enough that the users will not need to refer to the code. Usually the arguments are described in their order in the function call, starting with the input arguments. Use a bullet list or code format to put each argument on its own line.

To make a bullet list

```
%
% * meat      - a string: 'chicken' or 'beef'
% * condiment - a string: 'cilantro' or 'sprouts'
% * lunch     - a structure with each ingredient
%
```

which publishes as

- meat – a string: 'chicken' or 'beef'
- condiment – a string: 'cilantro' or 'sprouts'
- lunch – a structure with each ingredient

To make a code style list

```
%
%
% # meat      - a string: 'chicken' or 'beef'
% # condiment - a string: 'cilantro' or 'sprouts'
% # lunch     - a structure with each ingredient
%
```

which publishes as

```
meat      - a string: 'chicken' or 'beef'
condiment - a string: 'cilantro' or 'sprouts'
lunch     - a structure with each ingredient
```

Discuss any special requirements for the input arguments. The user will need to know if the input must be expressed in particular units, in a particular range, or as a particular type of array:

```
% ejectionFraction is from 0 to 1, not percentage.
% elapsedTimeSeconds must be one dimensional.
```

121. Describe Any Function Side Effects

Side effects are actions of a function other than assignment of the output variables. A common example is plot generation. Descriptions of any side effects should be included in the description comments block so that they appear in the reference page and are easy for the user to find.

122. Describe Any Custom Exceptions that May be Generated

This practice can help the user quickly interpret any runtime exceptions:

```
% An exception is thrown if altitude is
% negative.
```

123. Include Examples in the Header Comments

This practice is a useful supplement to the syntax lines. Some users find it easier to learn how to use a function from an example rather than the syntax section. Use monospaced text to display the example code. When you can write it compactly, provide a complete example with setup and output:

```
%% Example
%# lunch = pho('beef', 'cilantro')
```

which publishes as

Example

```
lunch = pho('beef', 'cilantro')
```

124. Include See also in the Header Comments

The see also related function list can provide useful links both to MATLAB distribution and locally developed functions. It allows the reader to easily compare related functions and to "discover" a similar function without knowing its name:

```
%% See also
% wrap
```

publishes as

See also

wrap

In some contexts, the MATLAB product will automatically generate hyperlinks to these function names.

125. Avoid Clutter in the Reference Page

It is common to include author, copyright, or other organization information in header comments. There should be a blank line between the main header comments and these comments so that they are not displayed in published output or in response to the help command.

126. Format Header Comments of classdef Files for the Help Browser

Many of the practices for formatting function header comments also apply to classdef files, but you can produce better results if you do not use the Publish feature. The Help on Selection feature provides useful class information, and it makes sense to include this information in the reference page. In this case, you select the class name, apply Help on Selection, and copy the HTML version of the displayed page to a file in your help folder.

Write a comment header for classdef files that includes the sections: description, syntax, examples, and see also. Because you do not use the Publish feature, its special comment-based markup does not work. The text in these sections (except for see also) will appear in monospaced font.

127. Clarify Subclass Methods

Use the description section of method comments to state any relationship with the corresponding superclass method. Use the verb "override" to indicate that a subclass method replaces a superclass method and does not call the superclass method; use the verb "extend" to indicate that a subclass method calls the superclass method (in addition to its own behavior).

Block Comments

Block comments are used to provide descriptions of files, code sequences, data structures, and algorithms. The multiline organization of block comments is usually easier to read than comments interspersed with code statements. They introduce sections and visually set off blocks of code. They provide a convenient place to describe the role of the code block and any special processing that is used. Block comments can also be useful for describing local constants defined in a block near the beginning of a function or script.

128. Indent Block Comments to Match Code

Block comments inside a function or method should precede the code they describe and be indented to the same level.

129. Place a Blank Line or Cell Break before a Block Comment

Use a blank comment line, a blank cell break line, or a section title to set the block comment off from the preceding code. These separators help the block comment look like a paragraph in the Editor:

```
%
% Use a global search to deal with local minima.
% Use the alpha algorithm because we have found
% problems with the faster beta algorithm.
```

A section title using a cell break before a block comment also publishes well. You must place a blank comment line between the section title and the block comment for correct publishing if you want to suppress the block comment. For example,

```
%% Minimize y within constraints on x.
%
% Use a global search to deal with local minima.
% Use the alpha algorithm because we have found
% problems with the faster beta algorithm.
```

publishes as

Minimize y within constraints on x.

Use a global search to deal with local minima. Use the alpha algorithm because we found problems with the faster beta algorithm.

Place a blank comment line between comment paragraphs. This helps the reader by chunking up the text for easier digestion.

130. Do Not Use Comment Blocks for Block Comments

A comment block is a block of text between the special characters %{ and %} instead of individual lines starting with % characters. For a comment block, the %{ and %} characters must appear on their own lines. Unfortunately, the Publish feature does not work with comment blocks. For example,

```
%{
Here is a comment block with some formatting.
* one
* two
* three
%}
```

The published output looks like

```
%{
Here is a comment block with some formatting.
* one
* two
* three
%}
```

instead of the individual comment line version

```
% %
% Here are comments with some formatting.
%
% * one
% * two
% * three
%
```

which publishes as

Here are comments with some formatting.

- one
- two
- three

If you do use block comments, then apply even left alignment in comment blocks to avoid a jagged distraction. Do not bother with aligned asterisks or other characters along the right side. They take too much time to maintain when the comment is changed.

131. Use Comment Block Syntax to Temporarily Bypass a Block of Code

It is easier to spot code that is commented out using comment blocks in the Editor, rather than the if 0 ... end construct. This may be the best use of comment blocks. Remove the code or the blocks before code release.

Interspersed or Inline Comments

Use interspersed comments to describe short implementation details. These include unusual or obtuse algorithms, workarounds, limitations, or code that should be reworked.

Interspersed comments tend to break up the flow of both code and comments. Using a block of comments is usually a better practice for longer descriptions. The block approach also publishes better.

132. Indent Comments with the Code Block

Avoid any other comment indentation that would break the layout of the code block. Short comments can appear on a single line indented to the level of the code that follows. If a comment cannot be written in a single line, then it should follow the block comment format.

133. Do Not Follow a Single-Line Comment with a Blank Line

The blank lines take up too much screen real estate. They also reduce the connection between the comment and the code.

134. Resolve TODO/FIXME Comments

You can add TODO or FIXME in a comment to generate an automated task list using the TODO Directory Report. Resolve and remove these comments before release. They should not be part of the released code or documentation.

Documentation Summary

Document files to meet the needs of the readers. Users need to know how to use the function, class, or method correctly without reading the code. The best way to support them is to provide well-formatted, informative reference pages that are consistent with standard practice and integrated into the Help browser. At a minimum, supply syntax, description, examples, and names of related functions.

The easiest way to produce these reference pages is to use the Publish feature with header comments that include the appropriate content and markup. Generating the reference pages directly from the code file makes it more likely that the two will be consistent. Include formatted comments in the same file as the code so that you can easily generate these pages.

Developers need to know what the code does, and how and why it does what it does. The best and most reliable documentation for them is clean code with good layout, naming, and logic. Informative and accurate comments in the code body are also a great help. Try to write the code so that working with it correctly does not depend on any constraints in the comments.

Write useful, not redundant, comments. Keep them consistent with code changes. Writing the comments while you code may help you write better code. Write comments in the code body so that they are easy for developers to read and associate with the relevant code. Assume that the code will be read in an editor. Use formatting that chunks the comments and code for easier scanning.

5.

Programming

Writing software requires making choices. If you choose the simplest and clearest option, then the code is more likely to be correct, useful, and sustainable. This advice was valid decades ago and is still relevant today. Modern agile development approaches emphasize simple code as a core value because it is quicker to develop, easier to test, and easier to modify.

General

135. Avoid Cryptic Code

There is a tendency among some MATLAB programmers to write code that is terse and even obscure. Perhaps they are inspired by Shakespeare's line: "Brevity is the soul of wit." Writing overly compact code can be a way to explore the features of the language. However, in almost every circumstance, clarity should be the goal. Do not confuse writing MATLAB code with cryptography.

Write code that is clear and readable by yourself and others. The way you put the program together is as important as what it does. Clear code is more likely to do what it is intended to do. Code that is difficult to understand and describe will also be difficult to write correctly, test, and maintain.

136. Avoid Off-By-One Mistakes

Off-by-one errors are all too common at variable boundary values. For example, interpolation code for an NTSC video frame might include the incorrect

```
0:480
```

Because an NTSC frame has 480 lines, this should be

```
1:480
```

or

```
0:479
```

or even better

```
nLines = 480;
1:nLines
```

137. Attend to NaN Results

If NaN is the result of a computation, then MATLAB by default does not issue an error or warning. You may want to issue your own. Write message identifiers so that these errors or warnings can be easily recognized.

138. Consider Using isfinite

Some computations produce Inf rather than NaN. If Inf will lead to issues with your code, then it may be best to screen for both results using isfinite rather than just isnan.

139. Use Programming Patterns or Idioms

See how others have dealt with the task. Most programming patterns have evolved from actual use, so they tend to be reliable and accurate. The best patterns are also well written and clear. Expect, however, that you will need to adapt a pattern to your specific use.

If the function you are writing has an interface similar to a standard MATLAB function or to one of your own functions, then its input and output arguments should be in the same format and order. Using familiar arguments in familiar order increases usability and readability. For example, if a function is similar to the minimization function `fminsearch`, then it should have similar input arguments in similar order: function handle, starting location, and options structure of optimization parameters.

If a function you are writing has similar functionality to a standard MATLAB function or to one of your own functions, then consider using the same code layout and organization. For example, many functions that compute scalars from array columns can be written in similar ways to support expected direction arguments and defaults.

Variables and Constants

A *variable* is a named reference whose value can be defined or changed in the code. A *constant* is a named reference whose value should not be changed after it is assigned. Many of the style considerations for variables also apply to constants.

140. Do Not Reuse Variable Names Unless Required by Memory Limitation

Enhance readability by ensuring all entities or concepts are represented uniquely. Reduce the chance of error from a misunderstood or no longer current definition of a variable. Also avoid changing the class of an existing variable; instead, improve readability and performance by using a new variable.

141. Beware of Mistyping Variable Names

Because MATLAB does not require variables to be declared, it is possible to unintentionally introduce a new variable by mistyping. Be particularly careful to avoid inconsistent capitalization in variable names. It is difficult to notice at a glance the difference between videoFrame and videoframe or Points and points. For example, here is a code snippet with inconsistent capitalization:

```
function points = dosomething(x, y)
points = zeros(length(x), 2);
    :
for i = 1:nPoints
        Points(i) = [x(i) y(i)];
end
```

In this example, the elements of the output variable points will always be zero because the variable name in the loop is mistyped as Points. In some cases of code like this, there may be no M-Lint error or warning, but the variable will not have the expected value.

142. Minimize the Use of Literal Numbers in Statements

Use named constants or variables instead of literal (hard-coded) numbers. If a number does not have an obvious meaning by itself, then the reader is not likely to understand its significance. Readability is enhanced by introducing a named constant or variable instead.

Named variables are also more maintainable. Almost all numbers in code are subject to possible change. Changing the value of a named value is easier than finding and changing the relevant occurrences of a literal number in a file.

Replace

```
for i = 1:640,
```

with

```
nColumns = 640;
for jColumn = 1:nColumns
```

If the number of columns in the example is also used within the for loop, then there is a maintenance issue when a literal is used. If the number of columns is changed, then all instances of the literal 640 would need to be located and changed.

143. Write Floating Point Values with a Digit Before the Decimal Point

This practice adheres to mathematical conventions for syntax. Also, 0.5 is more readable than .5; that is, it is not as likely to be read as the integer 5 or some other incorrect value.

Replace

```
THRESHOLD =.5;
```

with

```
THRESHOLD = 0.5;
```

144. Avoid Showing Excessive Decimal Places

Computers can produce values with a large number of decimal places, even when the underlying situation justifies only a few. Including an excessive number of decimal places can give a false sense of precision. Long numbers with many digits are also difficult to visually scan. There can easily be a mistake in an important digit that could be missed in the clutter of unimportant digits.

145. Avoid Mixing Units within a Program

In almost all cases, the variables and constants should have units that are either all SI (metric) or all U.S. Customary System. Avoid computations with mixed units unless they are simple conversions. Mixing MKS and CGS representations may be common in some domains. In these contexts, append a units suffix to any ambiguous variable name.

146. Use Caution with Floating Point Comparisons

The necessarily finite binary representation of real numbers in a computer can cause trouble, particularly in testing for equality, as in this example.

These values work as expected:

```
shortSide = 3;
longSide = 5;
otherSide = 4;
longSide^2 == (shortSide^2 + otherSide^2)
ans =
     1
```

but these do not:

```
scaleFactor = 0.01;
(scaleFactor*longSide)^2 ==   ...
((scaleFactor*shortSide)^2 + ...
(scaleFactor*otherSide)^2)
ans =
     0
```

A better approach is to test for a small difference:

```
small = eps*shortSide;
thisLongSide = scaleFactor*longSide;
thisShortSide = scaleFactor*shortSide;
thisOtherSide = scaleFactor*otherSide;
thisLongSide^2 - (thisShortSide^2 + ...
     thisOtherSide^2) < small
ans =
     1
```

147. Limit Boolean Variable Values to True or False

Boolean variables should assume only the logical values true or false. Avoid using character strings like yes/no or on/off. If desired, modify the variable name to include the positive form of one of these terms. Do not use true or false for the values of variables that are not Boolean.

Replace

```
safety = 'on'
```

with

```
safetyIsOn = true
```

148. Do Not Assume Array Size

Array sizes can change unexpectedly. Use end for indexing when possible.

Replace

```
nData = 10;
data(nData-3:nData)
```

with

```
data(end-3:end)
```

because the first two statements might be separated by code that at some point changes the size of the array data so that nData is no longer its length.

149. Use Appropriate Numerical Class Conversions

Be aware of how numerical data are converted to a different class. Usually, numerical type conversions should be done by explicit assignment rather than by promotion. This makes it clear to the reader what is going on and that the programmer is aware of what he or she is doing.

If the variable alpha is uint8, then replace the promotion

```
b = 1.0*alpha;
```

with an assignment

```
b = double(alpha);
```

150. Minimize the Use of Global Variables

The use of global variables makes software more difficult to read and understand. Because code anywhere in the software can change the value of the variable at any time, understanding the use of the global variable may entail understanding a large portion of the program.

Clarity and maintainability of functions benefit from explicit argument passing rather than use of global variables. In fact, the use of global variables makes it more difficult to isolate units of code for purposes of unit testing, thus global variables can directly contribute to lowering the quality of the code.

Some use of global variables can be replaced with the cleaner `persistent` declaration (within a function). The use of persistent variables has another advantage in that the `clear` command removes global but not persistent variables.

You can also use `setappdata` and `getappdata` to work with variables that have global availability:

```
setappdata(SharedHandle, 'thetaDegrees', 90)
thetaDegrees  = getappdata(SharedHandle,
                 'thetaDegrees')
```

An alternative, and better, strategy is to replace the global variable with a function, as in this prototype:

```
function out = globalproxy(in)
persistent inside
if nargin>0
    inside = in;
end
out = inside;
```

In this case, there is a relatively clear distinction in the code between *using* the variable (no input argument) and *defining* it (an input argument).

151. *Minimize the Use of Global Constants*

It can be convenient to use a constant that is defined once and used in multiple locations. This effect can be achieved by declaring the constant as global, but there is a price to pay. You must run the code that defines the constant before you can use it. Because the location of this code may not be obvious, you can also inadvertently and inconsistently define the constant in more than one location.

MATLAB does not have true constants. They are really variables that are, or should be, resistant to change. There are several strategies for working with constants that are used in more than one code module.

The recommended practice is to define constants that will be used in more than one module as functions. This reduces the likelihood of unintentional redefinition. Also, the constant name can be easily used in an expression. Using a function to define a constant is a common MATLAB practice. Use the standard convention for naming this function. The function definition would look like

```
function value = twopi
value = 2.0*pi;
```

and the usage would be

```
circumference = twopi*radius;
```

If execution speed is an issue, then you can use an anonymous function

```
circumference = @twopi*radius;
```

or make a local copy

```
twoPiConstant = twopi;
circumference = twoPiConstant*radius;
```

You could instead put constant definitions in a structure, but this practice is not common:

```
constants.twoPi = 2.0*pi;
```

with usage

```
circumference = constants.twoPi*radius;
```

You could use a property of an object as a constant. If you do not define a method that changes the property, then you have a true constant. However, it is best to access this property through a getter method rather than direct access, which makes its usage a bit cumbersome:

```
circumference = getTwoPi(C)*radius;
```

or

```
circumference = C.getTwoPi*radius;
```

152. Define Local Constants Only Once

Make it clear where the constants are defined in a module, and discourage unintentional redefinition. If a constant is used at only one location in a file, then define it just before it is used. Otherwise, define it near the top of the file.

153. Do Not Declare Unrelated Variables in a Single Line

You can make scanning for variable names easier by grouping them.

Replace

```
persistent   alpha, beta, triangle, square
```

with

```
persistent   alpha, beta
persistent   triangle, square
```

Character Strings

MATLAB is flexible in working with strings, but it can be slow. This is one of the few cases where considering speed early in the coding process is worthwhile.

154. Consider Using `strcmpi`

Often we want to ignore variations in capitalization when comparing strings. Using `strcmpi` is better than making two or more comparisons.

Replace

```
strcmp(reply, 'no') | strcmp(reply, 'No')
```

with

```
strcmpi(reply, 'no')
```

Switch/case constructs do not support case-insensitive comparisons using strcmpi, but you can use a cell array:

```
switch reply
    case {'no', 'No'}
```

155. Use `lower` or `upper` *When You Cannot Use* `strcmpi`

Most programmers use lowercase for comparison. This avoids two or more comparisons:

```
switch lower(reply)
    case 'no'
```

156. Use `isempty`

The clearest way to test whether a character string is empty is to use the `isempty` function.

Replace

```
isequal(a, '')   or   isequal(a, [])
```

with the easier-to-scan and type correctly

```
isempty(a)
```

The expressions

```
a=='' or a==[]
```

are not useful because they always return [].

Although it will work, avoid checking whether a string variable is empty by comparing its length to zero. The purpose of this statement is not as clear as simple use of isempty. Avoid

```
length(a)==0
```

157. Use fullfile

The fullfile function generates a path to a file that is system independent and flexible in dealing with embedded file separators.

Replace

```
thisFile = [disk, '\', directory, '\', filename];
```

with the more portable and easier-to-read

```
thisFile = fullfile(disk, directory, filename);
```

158. Compute with Numbers for Speed

Computing with index numbers can be much faster than working directly with character strings. In particular, working with date numbers is usually faster than working with date strings. If you write clearly, with good variable naming, this usage need not reduce readability.

159. Consider Using Character Arrays for Speed

The use of cell arrays for character strings can be easier to read, but working with character arrays can be faster. Try to limit this usage to cases that do not significantly reduce readability.

160. Consider Using unique

Take advantage of duplicate values in a string variable. Use the three output argument feature of unique:

```
[uniqueList, listIndex, uniqueListIndex] = ...
unique(list);
```

Using these optional output indices in subsequent computations can often be faster and more elegant than recomputing equivalent indices in additional statements.

Structures

161. Use Structures for Associated Data

Structures provide an easy way to keep associated data together. For example, you might have a set of gross domestic product (GDP) data by country and year. Instead of using variables GDP, country, and year, you would use a structure GDP with fieldnames value, country, and year. Using a structure can help keep the sizes of the fields consistent and also supports writing functions with fewer input arguments.

162. Use Structures for Metadata

Structures provide an easy way to keep related data together. For example, the results of an experiment could be kept in a structure so that you do not have to keep track of each relevant variable or parameter. This is particularly convenient if the results of several similar experiments are stored in files in a single directory:

```
Flight10702 =
        airSpeed: [1x10000 double]
    airSpeedUnit: 'MPH'
        altitude: [1x10000 double]
    altitudeUnit: 'feet'
```

```
       timeStep: 1
   timeStepUnit: 'sec'
      equipment: 'A7'
          pilot: 'John Glenn'
    description: 'practice'
      eventTime: [20x1 double]
       eventLog: {20x1 cell}
```

163. Organize a Structure Based on How It Will be Accessed

A structure is likely to be read more often than written, so organizing it for simple read access will produce cleaner code overall. Consider a structure with data for multiple flights. If the most frequent access is one flight at a time, then organize the structure as

```
Flight(nFlights).airspeed(nSamples)
```

If the most frequent access is all flights for one field at a time, then use a structure organized as

```
Flight.airspeed(nFlights, nSamples)
```

164. Put Structure Fields in a Helpful Order

MATLAB does not consider field order for functions like `isequal`, but using alphabetical ordering can make it easier for a reader to find a field in a structure display. You can use the `orderfields` function to provide a structure with fields in alphabetical order.

Some users prefer to order the data fields first, followed by the metadata fields. The order of the fields does not affect the format or speed of use. It is only a factor in readability.

165. Be Careful with Fieldnames

When you set the value of a structure field, MATLAB replaces the existing value if the field already exists or creates a new field if it does not. This can lead to unexpected results if the fieldnames are not consistent, for example, when a structure has field

```
Acme.source = 'CNN';
```

that you intend to update, but you type

```
Acme.sourceName = 'Bloomberg';
```

The structure will now have two fields. A less error-prone version would be

```
if isfield('Acme', 'sourceName')
    Acme.sourceName = 'Bloomberg';
else
    error('fieldset:name', 'Use a valid
    fieldname.')
end
```

This code snippet could also be generalized and written as a function for safer and more convenient use.

Another way to avoid this type of problem is to use an object rather than a structure. One of the benefits of object-oriented programming is resistance to unintentional field creation.

Cell Arrays

Cell arrays are very flexible and can hold any type of array. This flexibility can, however, lead to some confusion. The most important uses for cell arrays are for character strings, function arguments, and nonrectangular numerical arrays.

166. Consider Using Cell Arrays for Strings

Cell arrays of character strings can be more readable than character arrays, particularly if the strings have different lengths.

Indexing cell arrays is usually more direct than indexing character arrays.

You can count spaces to write

```
greetings = ['Hi    '; 'World']
```

or use the function

```
greetings = char('Hi', 'World')
```

However, in both cases, the indexing would be in the form

```
greetings(iLine,:)
```

With a cell array, you can write

```
greetings = {'Hi'; 'World'}
```

and index with the more direct

```
greetings{iLine}
```

167. Look Out for Cells within Cells

It can be easy to write

```
greetings{1} = {'Hi'};
```

when the desired statement is

```
greetings{1} = 'Hi';
```

or

```
Greetings(1) = {'Hi'};
```

The first statement will require unnecessarily complicated syntax for correct access of the character string.

168. Consider Using Cell Arrays for Ragged Arrays

Most arrays in MATLAB must have uniform numbers of rows and columns. If the elements in your data set do not have this rectangular shape, then you have two choices. You can use a padded array or a cell array.

If the data have a natural alignment such as uniformly spaced samples with some missing values, then use a NaN padded array.

If the data do not have a natural alignment, then use of a padded array may be misleading. In this case, use a cell array. Using a cell array will typically be slower than a NaN padded array, but you can use cell array functions for better performance.

Expressions

An expression consists of one or more operators and one or more operands or functions. Expressions are the building blocks of statements.

169. Write Short Expressions

To enhance readability, try to use less than seven elements in an expression. Look for opportunities to use explanatory intermediate variables. An expression like

```
isnan(thisValue)&(thisValue>=initialThreshold)
&~ismember(value,valueArray)
```

should be replaced by something like

```
valueIsPresent = ~isnan(thisValue);
valueIsValid = thisValue >= initialThreshold;
valueIsNew = ~ismember(thisValue, valueArray);
(valueIsPresent && valueIsValid && valueIsNew)
```

The latter version makes it easier to visually parse the overall expression into meaningful subexpressions and to see that the subexpressions are correct.

170. Put Numbers Before the Multiplication Operator

When a variable is multiplied by an explicit number, put the number before the operator and the variable name after. Because you should minimize the use of numbers within the body of code, this rule applies mostly when defining a variable that replaces a literal number.

Replace

```
twoPi = pi*2;
```

with

```
twoPi = 2*pi;
```

The reverse order is appropriate when the number is a numerator of a fraction:

```
fudgeFactor = peak*2/3;
```

171. Make the Denominator Clear

The scalar expressions

```
a/b*c
```

and

```
a*c/b
```

produce the same result, but the second form can be understood more quickly. Similarly,

```
a/b*c/d
```

is not as clear as

```
(a*c)/(b*d)
```

172. Use Parentheses

The MATLAB language has documented rules for operator precedence, but who wants to remember the details? If there might be any doubt, then use parentheses to clarify expressions. They are particularly helpful for extended logical expressions.

The expression

```
a == b&c
```

is evaluated as

```
(a == b) & c
```

although

```
a == (b & c)
```

may be the intent.

The expression

```
a*b/c*d
```

is evaluated as

```
((a*b)/c)*d
```

The intent may have been

```
(a*b)/(c*d)
```

If not, it would be better to write

```
a*b*d/c
```

173. Use a Clear Form for Relational Expressions

Relational expressions, including negations, can be difficult to understand. Strive to use positive expressions. You may be able to write a positive form by using the complementary operator.

Replace

```
~(iSample<maxSamples)
```

with

```
iSample>=maxSamples
```

174. Use && or || by Default for Scalar Operands

Use && or || by default, and put expressions in the best order for short circuiting to avoid errors, warnings, or unnecessary computation. Use

```
exist(a) && a>0
```

or

```
~isempty(a) && a>0
```

When the operands are not scalars, you must use & or | instead of the short circuiting operators.

Statements

A statement is a line or construct of executable code. Statements typically consist of one or more expressions. Most functions are sequences of statements.

175. Write Short Statements

Statements are easier to read when they are short. In particular, try to avoid unnecessary line wraps by introducing intermediate variables and short expressions.

176. Avoid Use of eval When Possible

Statements that involve eval tend to be harder to write correctly, more difficult to read, and slower to execute than alternatives. Use of eval does not support thorough checking by M-Lint. Statements that use eval can usually be improved by changing from commands to functions, or by using dynamic field references for structures with setfield and getfield.

Reduce use of `eval` by using the function form rather than the command form. The command form is more limited than the function form in working with arguments. The command form often requires a more cryptic statement than the function form. Replace

```
eval(['load August' int2str(index) '.mat'])
```

with

```
load(['August', int2str(index) '.mat']);
```

Also minimize the use of `evalin`. It should not be used to secretly pass values into functions. Use arguments instead.

Loops

Historically, MATLAB programmers have preferred to use vectorization instead of `for` loops to achieve better performance. Recent releases have brought considerable improvements in the execution speed of `for` loops, and they are becoming more common. Programmers with backgrounds in other languages will typically find code written with `for` loops more readable than code written with complicated vectorization.

177. Initialize Loop Variables Immediately Before the Loop

Initializing or preallocating the variables that are updated in a loop improves loop speed and helps prevent bogus values if the loop does not execute for all desired indices. Placing the initialization just before the loop makes it easier to see that the variables are initialized. This practice also makes it easier to copy the relevant code for use elsewhere. If a loop variable is not a double, then assign its type when you initialize it:

```
result = nan(nEntries,1);
for index = 1:nEntries
```

```
    result(index) = foo(index);
end
```

178. *Initialize Using* nan *or* false *Rather Than* zeros

Now that nan is available as a function, use it. Because zero can be a valid result of many computations, incomplete element computation is easier to detect when the array is initialized to nan:

```
aloha = nan(nRows, nColumns);
```

If the variable is Boolean, then initialize it using false. This practice prevents subsequent MATLAB code from interpreting zero as an invalid matrix index:

```
resultIsValid = false(nRows, nColumns);
```

179. *Do Not Change the Loop Index Variable Inside a Loop*

MATLAB captures the loop index variable for use in executing the loop. You can change the variable with the same name inside the loop, but the result may not be what you expect. In any case, changing the apparent value of the loop variable will confuse the reader.

180. *Minimize the Use of* break *in Loops*

This keyword is often unnecessary and should only be used if the code proves to have higher readability than a structured alternative, and it is well tested. A loop containing break will have more than one output path. This can be confusing. In nested loops with break statements, it is not always obvious which statement will be executed next.

Replace

```
fid = fopen('fft.m','r');
s = '';
```

```
while ~feof(fid)
   line = fgetl(fid);
   if isempty(line), break, end
   s = strvcat(s,line);
end
```

with

```
fid = fopen('fft.m','r');
s = '';
textLine = '*';
while ~feof(fid) && ~isempty(textLine)
   textLine = fgetl(fid);
   s = strvcat(s,textLine);
end
```

181. Minimize the Use of continue in Loops

This keyword is often unnecessary and should only be used if the code proves to have higher readability than a structured alternative. The following example reads a text file of unknown length:

```
fid = fopen('magic.m','r');
count = 0;
while ~feof(fid)
    line = fgetl(fid);
    if isempty(line) | strncmp(line,'%',1)
        continue
    end
    count = count + 1;
end
```

This code can easily be written without continue by changing the sense of the if statement expressions:

```
fid = fopen('magic.m','r');
count = 0;
```

```
while ~feof(fid)
    textLine = fgetl(fid);
    count = update(count, textLine);
end
fclose(fid)
```

together with the function

```
function count = update(count, textLine)
if ~isempty(textLine) &&
    ~strncmp(textLine,'%',1)
    count = count + 1;
end
```

This version also renames the variable line to avoid confusion with the function of the same name.

182. Avoid Unnecessary Computation within Loops

Save execution time and make debugging easier by avoiding repeated computations that are not needed.

Replace

```
for iRow = 1:nRows
    for jCol = 1:nColumns
        term(iRow, jCol) = sum(x(iRow,:)) +
        sum(x(:,jCol));
    end
end
```

with the cleaner and faster

```
for iRow = 1:nRows
    rowSum = sum(x(iRow,:));
    for jCol = 1:nColumns
        term(iRow, jCol) = rowSum +
        sum(x(:,jCol));
    end
end
```

183. Be Careful of Infinite while Loops

Code blocks using while can loop indefinitely if the exit condition is not written well. For example, an equality test involving floating point numbers may never pass. This loop does not terminate:

```
a = 30;
b = 0.1;
while a~=0
    a = a-b;
end
```

This one does:

```
a = 30;
b = 0.1;
while a>=0
    a = a-b;
end
```

184. Be Careful of Count Errors in while Loops

It is easy to write code like

```
count = 1;
value = 3;
decrement = 1;
while value>0
    value = value-decrement;
    count = count+1;
end
```

This produces a count value of 4. Because the desired value is probably 3, the code should be

```
count = 0;
value = 3;
decrement = 1;
```

```
while value>0
    value = value-decrement;
    count = count+1;
end
```

Conditionals

Conditional or selection constructs using `if` or `switch` establish blocks of statements that are always done together and in sequence. Good use of these constructs is very important for correctness and understandability.

185. *Avoid Complicated Conditional Expressions*

Introduce intermediate logical variables to reduce complexity. By assigning logical variables to expressions, the program gets automatic documentation. The construction will be easier to read and debug.

Replace

```
if (value>=lowLimit)&(value<=highLimit)& ...
~ismember(value, knownValues);
  :
end
```

with

```
isValid = (value>=lowLimit) && ...
          (value<=highLimit);
isNew   = ~ismember(value, knownValues);
if (isValid && isNew)
  :
end
```

186. *In General, Include an* `else` *Statement with* `if`

The `else` block provides an opportunity to deal with an alternative or unexpected value.

Replace

```
if iState<=50
   disp(state(iState))
end
```

with

```
nStates = 50;
if iState <= nStates
   disp(state(iState))
else
   error('Keep iState smaller than nStates+1.')
end
```

187. Put the Normal Branch in the if Part

Put the normal branch of an if statement first unless placing the special case first makes the construct more easily understandable. This practice improves readability by preventing lengthy special cases from obscuring the normal path of execution. For example, code that reads a file might be clearer if the code block that reads the file is placed before the code block that is executed if the file is not successfully opened:

```
fid = fopen(fileName);
if (fid >= 0)
   :
else
   :
end
```

188. Avoid Unnecessary if Constructs

You can often replace code such as

```
if expression
   value = true;
else
   value = false;
end
```

with

```
value = expression;
```

189. Use a Practical Order for `elseif` Conditions

When the selection construct has many choices, readability is improved if the choices are in some type of order. Typical ordering includes numerical order as in 0, 1, 2 or alphabetical order for character strings.

190. Avoid Unnecessary `elseif` Blocks

A selection construct with apparent but unnecessary choices can confuse the reader. You can often clarify the construct by replacing literal numbers with named values.

Replace

```
if hours < 40
    pay = regular(hours);
elseif hours > 40
    pay = overtime(hours);
elseif hours == 40
    pay = regular(hours)
else
    error('Bad condition')
end
```

with

```
normalHours = 40;
if hours <= normalHours
    pay = regular(hours);
else
    pay = overtime(hours);
end
```

191. *Avoid Unnecessary Levels of Nesting in Control Structures*

Code within `if` or `switch` constructs can become messy if the cases are not well designed or if additional conditions are added to the original version. Reorganization can improve readability. Removal of duplicated code can also make it easier to maintain consistency while modifying. The confusing code

```
if heated
if usage < 500
bill = 0.9*(2+0.1);
else
bill = 0.9*(5+0.2);
end
else
if usage < 500
bill = 0.95*(2+0.1);
else
bill = 0.95*(5+0.2);
end
end
```

can be rewritten more clearly as

```
if heated
    scale = 0.90;
else
    scale = 0.95;
end
if usage < 500
    base = 0.2;
    rate = 0.1;
else
    base = 5;
    rate = 0.2;
end
bill = scale * (base+rate*usage);
```

192. *Try to Simplify Nested* if *Constructs*

Use of functions combined with conditions can reduce the need for nested if statements.

Replace

```
if x <= y
if x <= z
smallest = x;
else
smallest = z;
end
else
if y <= z
smallest = y;
else
smallest = z;
end
end
```

with

```
if x <= y
    smallest = min(x,z);
else
    smallest = min(y,z);
end
```

or

```
smallest = min([x, y, z]);
```

193. *Avoid the Conditional Expression* if 0

This expression is sometimes used to temporarily bypass a block of code. Do not use it; instead, use block comments. Do not release code containing if 0.

194. *Include* otherwise *with* switch *Statements*

Leaving otherwise out is a common error, which can lead to unexpected results because none of the cases may be executed. Use a construct such as

```
switch (condition)
    case abc
        :
    case def
        :
    otherwise
        :
end
```

195. *Consider Using a Cell Array to Simplify a* switch *Construct*

You can often use a cell array to consolidate selections that can be handled with a single block of code. Replace

```
switch lower(day)
    case 'mon'
        dayNo = 2;
    case 'tue'
        dayNo = 3;
    otherwise
        error('Bad day')
end
```

with the more flexible

```
allDays = {'mon', 'tue'};
index = strcmpi(day, allDays);
if ~empty(index)
    dayNo = find(index);
else
    error('Having a bad day')
end
```

or

```
allDays = {'mon', 'tue'};
switch day
    case allDays
        index = strcmpi(day, allDays);
        dayNo = find(index);
    otherwise
        error('Having a bad day')
end
```

Unlike the first version, these latter versions can be compactly generalized by

```
allDays = {'sun', 'mon', 'tue', 'wed', 'thu', ...
'fri', 'sat'};
```

196. Use if *When the Condition is Most Clearly Written as an Expression*

The if construct executes statements when the if or elseif expression is true. These include explicit or implied logical or relational expressions. The if construct can be used for both inequality and equality. An example would be code to determine the location of a number as above, inside, or below the bounds of an interval, with all numbers as variables.

197. Use switch *When the Condition is Most Clearly Written as a Value*

The switch construct only evaluates for equality. Use the switch construct when a single expression (the switch expression) is compared with a series of case values. Its best use is in comparing character strings or numerical variables.

198. *When Either* if *or* switch *Can Work, Use the More Readable One*

There is possible overlap in the usages of if and switch. Use the construct that provides cleaner, easier-to-read code.

Logical Functions

199. *Use* `logical` *to Cast Variables*

Use the function `logical` to cast variables that will be used for logical indexing. Some computations or functions produce results that consist of only one or zero values that could be used as indices. In some cases, MATLAB interprets a zero that is intended to be logical as an invalid numerical index. Use the logical function to avoid these problems. For example,

```
>> A = [1 2; 3 4];
>> A(logical(eye(2)))
ans =
     1
     4
```

but

```
>> A(eye(2))
??? Subscript indices must either be real
positive integers or logicals.
```

200. *Use* `true` *or* `false` *Functions and Values*

Use the `true` or `false` function to define or predefine a logical variable:

```
isValid = true(nRows, nColumns)
```

is faster and easier to read than

```
isValid = logical(ones(nRows, nColumns))
```

Similarly, use true or false values such as `while true` rather than `while 1` for an indeterminate `while` loop.

201. *In General Use* `isequal` *Rather Than* `==`

The major advantage of the isequal function is that it works with variables that have different sizes, which == does not.

Both isequal and == work with variables that are the same size. The isequal function yields the single overall result of the comparison, which is usually the desired result. The == operator yields a result the same size as the variables. You could use all with == to produce an overall result, but using isequal is simpler.

Replace

```
[1 1] == [1 1 1]
```

which produces an error, with

```
isequal([1 1], [1 1 1])
```

In general, replace

```
[1 1 1]==[1 1 0]
```

which produces three values, with

```
isequal([1 1 1], [1 1 0])
```

which produces one value.

Vectorization

202. Be Thoughtful with Vectorization

Older versions of MATLAB had significant performance problems with code written in loops. Newer versions often provide equivalent, or even better, performance with loops as with vectorized code. This is especially true when the computed variables are preallocated and Just-In-Time acceleration can be applied to the code. Vectorization is also less capable with large data variables because of memory limit issues.

Most MATLAB developers understand straightforward vectorization, but many of us bog down at the more arcane examples. Vectorization does have a good home in linear algebra applications. Even in those cases, it can benefit from explanatory comments for nonspecialists.

203. *Use* `repmat`

Use `repmat` to replicate a subarray to construct a larger array, unless speed is a problem. The old techniques

```
B = A(:, ones(1:nColumns));
```

or

```
B = A*ones(1, nColumns);
```

are effective and may be faster than `repmat`, but they are more difficult to read and less flexible than

```
B = repmat(A, 1, nColumns);
```

Functions

Structuring code, both among and within files, is essential to making it understandable, usable, and maintainable. Thoughtful partitioning and organizing increase the value of the code while and after it is developed. The use of functions is a key element of structuring procedural code.

204. *Modularize*

Decompose major tasks into subtasks. The best way to write a big program is to assemble it from well-designed small pieces (usually functions). This approach enhances readability, understanding, and testing by reducing the amount of text that must be read to see what the code is doing. Small well-designed functions are also more likely to be usable in other applications. Small focused functions are easier to test and modify than complicated ones.

Code longer than two editor screens is a candidate for partitioning into functions or subfunctions. Keeping related information together on the same editor screen lets you see certain types of problems and fix them right away. Displaying an entire logical unit on one screen also makes it easier for the reader to mentally organize and understand the code.

205. Write Code as Functions When Possible

Functions modularize computation by using internal variables that are not part of the base workspace. They tend to be cleaner, more flexible, and better designed than scripts. The main role of scripts is in development because they provide direct visibility of variable dimensions, types, and values.

206. Write Simple Functions

Write functions that do one thing and do it well. Try to write functions simple enough to describe in no more than two sentences. The goal is to achieve capability without complexity. Avoid multiblade utility functions that require complicated interfaces. If a combination of multiple tasks is appropriate, then the individual tasks should be coded as helper functions or subfunctions.

207. Design for Loose Coupling

Every function should hide something; that is, it should perform a task that is not intertwined with other code. A function has loose coupling if it interacts with other code only through input and output arguments. Using well-defined interfaces is key to achieving reliable, understandable, and adaptable code.

Tight coupling also leads to unit test problems because the module under test requires additional external context. It also reduces extensibility and reusability. Furthermore, tight coupling allows error propagation and can lead to a chain of failures.

208. Use Subfunctions Appropriately

A function used by only one other function can be packaged as a subfunction in the same file. Keeping the code in one file can make it easier to understand and maintain.

MATLAB allows subfunction access from outside the main function file using a function handle. External access to subfunctions is a sign of undesirable tight coupling. If external access is required, then convert the subfunctions to functions unless a single file is required for portability.

Aim for loose coupling between functions and their subfunctions. A subfunction should not have to change just because function input arguments change. The function input arguments should not have to change if you change the subfunction implementation.

209. Hide Implementation Details

When possible, design the function so that the internal implementation of its task can be changed without changing the interface arguments. That way changes to the function will not ripple out into other code.

210. Write for High Cohesion

In a function with high cohesion, most of the code is related to one task or a small number of related tasks. Low cohesion leads to unnecessary complexity, loss of readability, and unlikely reusability.

An example of low cohesion would be a function that computes many different statistical parameters from a data set such as mean, median, mode, standard deviation, shape parameters, quantiles, max, min, and frequency. It is better to split this functionality among several routines, with each computing only one or a few related parameters.

211. Use Existing Functions

Developing a new function that is correct, readable, and reasonably flexible can be a significant task. Using an existing function that provides some or all required functionality is likely to be more effective. You can also use existing functions as prototypes or starting points for your code.

212. Eliminate Overlapping Functions

If you find functions that perform similar tasks with similar interfaces, then consider combining them into a single function. If appropriate, this function can have subfunctions to capture code for detailed differences in the tasks.

213. Provide Some Generality in Functions

Functions should usually be flexible enough to accept appropriate input variables as scalars, vectors, and arrays of two dimensions when these are likely to be used. Functions with input arguments that commonly have more than one representation should work with all of them. For example, image processing functions should at least work with `uint8` and `double` input variables.

214. Write a Function At One Level of Abstraction

Your code is more readable and more likely to be reusable when you program a function at a consistent level of abstraction. Simple abstractions allow easily digested changes in implementation. They can also help clarify the role and organization of the code.

Mixed levels often occur in selection constructs where some paths call other functions and some contain detailed statements. An example of code with more than one level of abstraction is

```
function y = consolidate(x, action)
switch action
    case 'sum'
        y = sum(x);
    case 'first'
        nRows = size(x,1);
        if nRows==1
            y = x(1);
        else
            y = x(1,:)
        end
end
```

If you make first a function, you can get more readable code at a single level of abstraction:

```
function y = consolidate(x, action)
switch action
    case 'sum'
        y = sum(x);
    case 'first'
        y = first(x);
end
```

215. Write Convenience Functions

If you code even simple tasks in functions, then you can assign them function handles and treat them consistently with related functions. A simple example of a convenience function compatible with a basic form of standard functions like sum or mean is

```
function y = first(x)
y = x(1,:)
```

You can then make a function handle to use the same way as standard function handles.

```
hFirst = @first;
```

Using this function, you can rewrite `consolidate` as

```
function y = consolidate(x, fHandle)
y = fHandle(x);
```

216. Make Interaction Clear

A function interacts with other code through input and output arguments and global variables. The use of arguments is almost always clearer and better than the use of global variables.

217. Name All Input Arguments

Avoid literal numbers when calling functions. The meaning of a number is usually less clear than the meaning of a named variable. Changing code that uses named variables is easier than changing code that has literal numbers. Replace

```
foo(alpha, 2)
```

with

```
foo(alpha, flavor)
```

A literal number is acceptable in conventional uses such as a dimension argument.

218. Write Boolean Functions to Return `true` or `false`

Avoid other return values that might confuse the user or maintainer, such as yes/ no or on/off.

219. Make Logical Output and Function Name Consistent

The output of a logical function should be true if the function name implies true when the condition is met. For the function

```
valueIsInRange = isinrange(value)
```

the output variable `valueIsInRange` should be true when the value is in range.

220. Minimize Input Flag Arguments

The common practice of using 0 or 1 as an input flag argument is concise but problematic. It means that the function does more than one thing. It is not obvious which value of the argument selects which option. It is not obvious which option is the default. Some better alternatives are as follows: Write two functions. Use a parameter/value pair. Use a function handle argument.

For example, the `mad` function in the Statistics Toolbox computes either the mean or the median absolute deviation using syntax

```
mad(x)
mad(x,0)
mad(x,1)
```

The computed function output would be easier to understand using

```
medianabsdeviation(x)
```

and

```
meanabsdeviation(x)
```

or

```
mad(x, 'estimator', 'median')
```

or

```
mad(x, @median)
```

221. Write Arguments in Useful Order

Consider the order of input and output function arguments, especially for optional arguments. If the input argument `a` is specified more often than b, or b is optional, then write the function as foo(a,b) rather than foo(b,a). If the output argument c is used more often than d or is needed to compute d, then write the function as [c, d] = foo rather than [d, c] = foo.

222. Use Lazy Evaluation

Avoid computing unneeded variables. Secondary outputs should only be computed if the user calls the function with arguments for them, unless the secondary outputs are computed as a natural part of the computing the primary output.

Use nargout to determine whether secondary outputs must be computed.

```
function [c, d] = foo(a)
% Compute c.
if nargout>1
    % Compute d.
    ...
end
```

223. Make Input and Output Arrays Consistent

Functions that produce output arrays of the same type and size as the input arrays should usually arrange those output arrays in the same orientation as the input. Do not turn columns into rows casually.

224. Use a Structure to Replace a Long List of Function Arguments

Usability of a function decreases as the number of arguments grows, especially when some arguments are optional. The arguments must be provided in order, and this order is often not obvious. The rules of the arguments may be unclear.

Consider using structures whenever the number of arguments exceeds four.

Structures can allow a change to the number of values passed to or from the function that is compatible with existing external code, particularly other functions. For example one function may use fields a, b, c, of a structure, whereas another function uses fields a, b, d. Using a structure may be easier than keeping track of individual variables, especially if a function changes to use additional variables.

225. Consider an Options Structure

Some tasks, such as optimization, require a number of operational parameters. Using an options structure as an input argument can simplify the function call. A structure is easier to parse than a string of parameter-value pairs. It can also provide a convenient way to define modifiable default parameters. You can establish your preferred values once and use them in many places. If the same options are used for more than one function, then it is easier to keep them consistent if they are in a structure.

Consider writing a function that establishes the structure with default values that can be modified. You can also use it to constrain parameter values that are input as arguments to be within validity limits.

226. Consider varargin *and* varargout

When a function accepts an arbitrary number of inputs, use varargin. It is often better to use the inputParser object than to write your own code to handle a variable number of inputs. The inputParser is particularly convenient to deal with parameter-value pairs. When a function accepts an arbitrary number of outputs, use varargout. Note that the output arguments will be in a cell array.

227. Use Parameter-Value Pairs for Optional, Unordered Input Arguments

The input arguments of standard functions are listed in order. This can be inconvenient when some arguments are unneeded based on preceding arguments or when the user may not remember argument order. Parameter-value pairs make it easier to deal with these situations.

With an appropriate function definition, the order-dependent usage

```
pattern = order(customer, cSize, color, form)
```

can be replaced with an order-independent version, which can be used as

```
pattern = order(customer, 'cSize','large',
'color', 'red', 'form','diagonal');
```

or

```
pattern = order(customer, 'cSize','large',
'form', 'diagonal', 'color', 'red');
```

228. In General, Use Caller Variable Names Consistent with the Function Argument Names

When calling the function

```
function foo(alpha, beta)
```

use

```
foo(alpha, beta)
```

or

```
foo(thisAlpha, thisBeta)
```

as long as the variable names are meaningful in both the function and calling code contexts. This practice makes it easier to quickly scan the code and match the variables to the arguments.

229. Define Imports Where They are Easy to Find

It can be convenient to import functions that are in namespace packages. Place import statements in a block near the beginning of the function.

230. Use Anonymous Functions Rather Than Inline Functions

These are both ways to create and use very short functions without making them subfunctions or stand-alone functions. Anonymous functions generate function handles rather than function definitions. They are more flexible than inline functions and more likely to be supported in future releases. If the anonymous function definition requires a line wrap or is too cryptic, then it should be written as a function, subfunction, or nested function instead.

231. Use Function Handles

Use function handles rather than inline functions or function name strings in functions that use input arguments referring to functions ("function functions") when you can. Function handles have the advantage that they can be used outside the usual scope and more directly than function name strings. Replace code that would use

```
foo(x, y, 'compare')
```

with code that would use

```
foo(x, y, @compare)
```

232. Avoid Including Hidden Side Effects

Hidden side effects confuse the reader about what the function will actually do. Side effects that only sometimes occur are even more problematic. An example of a function with a nonobvious side effect is `hist`. It returns the histogram as a variable if there is an output argument. If there is not an output argument, then `hist` makes a plot as a side effect.

233. Refactor

Refactoring means changing the internals of an existing code module for better design without changing its external behavior. Refactoring increases adaptability by decreasing complexity. Many of us write functions during development that become too long and include redundancies. Refactor this code.

When refactoring you would typically

- Replace an explicit number with a named constant or variable.
- Replace a poor identifier name with a better one.
- Extract a block of code and convert it to a function.
- Replace duplicate code with a function.
- Remove misleading comments.

Best practices for refactoring include

- Make only one change at a time.
- Run tests after each change.
- Use version control.

Input and Output

234. Write Input Functions

Data file input format and content are often messy and subject to change. Localizing the code that reads input improves maintainability. Avoid mixing input code with computation other than preprocessing code in a single function. Mixed-purpose functions are unlikely to have clean, stable interfaces.

Consider storing input data in a mat file with named variables for multiple processing accesses.

An easy way to prototype an input function is to use the Desktop Import Data feature. The code generated by this feature can serve as the base for development.

235. Provide Some Input Validity Checking

You can improve the reliability of many functions by checking the type and range of numerical input, as well as the validity of character strings. This is especially important for more general-purpose functions.

Invalid input can easily lead to an error that stops execution. Validity checking allows more graceful error handling. The appropriate amount of validity checking is a judgment call, depending on expected use. The `inputParser` and the `validatesttributes` and `validatestring` functions are very helpful for validity checking.

There is an old saying in software development: "Garbage in, garbage out." This attitude and practice is no longer acceptable. If the input is not as expected, then produce an exception, error, or warning as appropriate. If execution should continue, then set the output variables to a testable value such as NaN, blank, or empty.

236. Expect NaN Values in Data

NaN is often used for missing data. If a NaN is encountered in data, then try to work around it. You may want to use the `nan*` functions in the Statistics Toolbox or write your own. Often it is useful to use `any(isnan(x))` to quickly screen for the presence of NaN entries.

237. Use `feof` for Reading Files

Do not depend on simply counting an expected number of lines or data entries when reading input data files. This can easily lead to end-of-file errors or incomplete input. A better approach is to read until end of file. Code for this approach can be as simple as

```
while ~feof(fileId)
   textLine(iLine) = fgetl(fileId);
end
```

A data input function should usually return the number of lines or values read, with code such as

```
iLine = 0;
while ~feof(fileId)
   textLine(iLine) = fgetl(fileId);
   iLine = iLine+1;
end
```

238. Make Output Modules

Output file requirements are subject to change without notice. Avoid mixing output code with computation in a single function. Mixed-purpose functions are unlikely to be reusable.

239. Format Output for Easy Use

If the output will most likely be read by a human, then make it self-descriptive and easy to read. Present displayed or printed output in a consistent manner. Apply informative headings and titles.

If the output is more likely to be read by software than a person, then make it easy to automatically parse. If both uses are important, then make the output easy to parse, and write a formatter function to produce a human readable version.

240. Provide for Automation

Enable automated data processing by using number and date conventions in filenames. You can easily generate filenames such as data101, data102, etc., in a loop. Similarly, you can generate data_2000–07–01, data_2000–07–02, etc. You can also access multiple data folders when you have made the folder names easy to generate or select.

If the filenames are not in a specific numerical or alphabetical order, then you can use the `dir` function to collect the data filenames that are present. Write something like

```
d = dir ('*.dat');
nFiles = length(d);
for iFile = 1:nFiles
    data = load(d(iFile).name);
    :
end
```

Classes and Objects

For most of its existence, MATLAB has been a procedural language. Useful object-oriented capability has been added in recent releases. The object-oriented approach is especially helpful for problems where objects can effectively represent entities, for example, figures or graphical user interfaces. Many of the good programming practices for functions also apply to classes.

Use of objects for working with large amounts of data is controversial. Well-designed objects can reduce the likelihood of errors in processing, but they can introduce undesirable overhead. Classes that serve only as data containers without significant methods might be better replaced with structures.

241. Keep Classes Simple

Simple classes are easier to design, code, document, read, and understand. Classes that try to do too much cause problems in testing and use. The smaller the public interface of a class, the easier it is to learn.

One of the major benefits of object-oriented programming is that it encourages serious thought about which data belong together and what will be done with them. If a class seems too big, then refactor it into smaller, simpler classes. Replace a classes such as

```
Business
```

with classes such as

```
Product
Employee
Customer
```

and so on.

If a method is not needed, then do not include it. Do not include a method for functionality that can be reasonably achieved with existing methods. You will find it much easier to add a method later than to take one out.

If you have methods

```
credit
debit
```

then you may not need

```
transaction
```

242. Avoid Classes with Ambiguous Overlap

The reader should have a good idea about the meaning of a class without having to wonder about the difference between two or more classes.

If both

```
CustomerInfo and CustomerData
```

are classes, then try to replace them with a single class

```
Customer
```

243. *Construct Valid Objects*

In object-oriented programming, the constructor method is a contract with the users of the object. It tells them everything that is required to make a valid object. If the requirements are met, then the constructor must create a valid object. In particular, it must create all properties that can be accessed by its get-related methods.

If your Client class has properties

```
priority, address
```

then you need to have a constructor method such as

```
function ThisClient = Client(priority, address)
Client.priority = priority;
Client.address = address;
```

If the constructor allows an incomplete set of property values in its input argument list, then it must create valid default values for the undefined properties. These default values can be empty or NaN only if they are valid for these properties.

If you write a constructor such as

```
function ThisClient = Client(priority)
if nargin>0
    Client.priority = priority;
end
```

then you need to set a default value such as

```
properties
    priority = nan;
end
```

244. *Follow Constructor Conventions*

If the constructor is called with no input variables, then return an error unless you can construct a valid object. If the input is a list of property values or a parameter-value list, then return an error unless you can construct a valid object from the input variables. If the only input variable is an object of the same class, then return it. Constructing classes with this behavior makes it easier to write methods that support appropriate flexibility in input variables without leading to problems in use.

Write a constructor something like

```
function ThisClient = Client(priority)
if nargin>0
    ThisClient.priority = priority;
else
    error('Supply an input argument')
end
end
```

245. Define Small, Simple Methods

Small methods are easier to test and understand than complicated methods. A method should perform only one task, and you should be able to define it in a sentence or two. If the task does not have a simple definition, then split it into two tasks and write two methods. Even if these methods are only called in one context, they are likely to be easier to read, understand and test than one large conglomerate method.

A large method such as

```
processSignal
```

should be replaced with smaller methods

```
removeBias
detectArrival
```

246. Write Methods That You Can Unit Test

As with functions, write methods with low coupling. Write most methods as functions rather than parts of the classdef file so that you can test them easily. This practice will also keep the `classdef` file short and easy to read. The constructor and protected methods must be in the `classdef` file. Other methods should be functions in a private or @ directory.

247. Do Not Write a Method That Can Produce an Invalid Property

If a method assigns a value to a property, then it must assign a valid value. For example, if a property must be positive, then no method or method input variable should be able to make it negative. This practice is particularly an issue for set methods and public properties.

248. Avoid Incomplete Public Methods

Do not write a method that can produce inconsistent properties. This can occur if the method can change only one property without changing closely linked properties. For example, if date is represented in year, month, and day properties, then do not write a method that can change only one of them. In some cases, careful property definition or attribute choice can reduce the likelihood of incomplete public methods.

In this example, you could write

```
properties
    dateNumber
end
```

or

```
properties (SetAccess = private)
    year
    month
    day
end
```

You would then write a public method such as `changeDate` that would change the linked properties as needed.

249. Try to Make Properties Private

By default, MATLAB makes properties public with public get and set methods. The recommended object-oriented practice is to make properties private or protected whenever possible because encapsulation is a guiding principle for object-oriented design. The use of public properties reduces encapsulation because it negates data and implementation hiding.

If a class computes age from birthday, then use

```
properties (SetAccess = private)
    age
end
```

or possibly

```
properties (SetAccess = private, ...
            GetAccess = private)
    age
end
```

The disadvantage of private properties is that they cannot be used directly with the usual MATLAB array indexing. You may decide to keep some properties public to maintain this compatibility.

For a public property, you can simply use standard indexing and write

```
Stocks.price(1, 1:3) = 0;
```

For a private property, you would need an access function

```
price = Stocks.getPrice;
price(1, 1:3) = 0;
Stocks.setPrice(price);
```

The code using a public property is familiar to MATLAB programmers and more compact. The code using a private property supports encapsulation and provides an opportunity for argument variable checking, for example, to constrain the array indexing to be within the current array size.

250. Do Not Expose Properties with Behavior

Use a method to change a property that has behavior. Allowing direct access to the property can work, but this is likely to mislead the user. For example, the day of the month might be a property. Changing it may also require changing the month.

Replace access such as

```
Market.dayOfMonth = Market.dayOfMonth+1;
```

or

```
set(get(Market.dayOfMonth)+1)
```

with a method that can be used as

```
incrementday(Market,1)
```

or better

```
Market.incrementday(1)
```

251. Avoid Writing Methods with Many Input Arguments

Consolidate the input arguments into fewer, higher-level variables (e.g., structures) or write smaller methods. As with functions, methods with many arguments are difficult to understand and use.

252. Validate Method Argument Values

Do not trust that the variables passed as input arguments will be exactly as expected. In general, check the input values for type and range.

For example,

```
function ThisPackage = setweight(ThisPackage,
value)
if value<0
    error('Use a nonnegative weight')
end
ThisPackage.weight = value;
end
```

253. Check for a Property's Existence Before Using It

Methods, especially public methods that involve get access, should protect themselves against possible missing or invalid properties. This problem can easily occur as the result of incomplete constructor or setter methods.

254. Refactor Repeated Code Into Methods

It is difficult to keep repeated method code consistent with the all but inevitable changes. Removing duplication is a crucial element of refactoring. Writing a separate or private method can ease this maintenance. If you find yourself copying and pasting among methods of a class, then consider cutting and pasting to a new method instead.

255. Overload Standard Functions When Possible

Using the standard MATLAB function makes it easier to recognize the meaning of the method and to avoid misspellings in use. Most standard functions have been used extensively and are likely to have fewer defects than new code. If the Sales.mean method computes the mean of a numerical array, then overload the standard mean function rather than writing a custom method to perform the task.

256. Avoid Unconventional Usage of Overload Names

Using a standard function name for an overload that does something different will confuse the reader. For example,

```
Amplitude.add
```

should perform an addition, not a concatenation or some other operation.

257. Do not Overload && or ‖

You will lose the ability to short circuit expression evaluation. Short circuiting is valuable for both error reduction and performance improvement.

258. Do not Get Carried Away with Inheritance

One level of inheritance is usually the best practice. The MATLAB language allows multiple levels of inheritance, that is for example, defining a class as a subclass of a subclass of a superclass. This practice can be difficult to design, maintain, and understand.

The MATLAB language also allows multiple inheritance, that is, defining a class as a subclass of two or more superclasses. This practice can also be difficult to design , maintain, and understand. In particular, changing one of the superclasses can lead to conflicts that are awkward to resolve.

259. Place Method Functions in Folders Consistently

Functions that are overloads and use the object as an input argument must be in the @ folder. Functions that do not use the object as an input argument must be on the MATLAB path, typically in the parent of the @ folder. Functions that are not overloads but use the object as an input argument could in principle be in either folder. Place them in the @ folder to help avoid function shadowing.

260. Use Java Syntax for Java Methods

In general, use the standard Java style to invoke methods of Java objects:

```
Chart.setYLabel('$')
```

You can also use the MATLAB syntax:

```
set(Chart, 'YLabel', '$')
```

Avoid using mixed syntax:

```
setYLabel(Chart, '$')
```

Exceptions, Errors, and Warnings

261. Use Appropriate Error Handling

Errors happen. When they do, handle them based on severity and context. MATLAB provides several choices for dealing with errors:

Let the error halt the program.
Issue an error message.
Return an error code.
Return NaN or [].
Generate a warning.

In general, use the functions `error` or `warning` depending on severity. Do not use the function `disp` to issue errors or warnings.

262. Prepare for Errors

Both data and code are potential error sources. Write defensive code to check for errors early and often. Try to provide a graceful way to deal with errors. In general, errors should be caught in low-level routines and fixed or passed on to higher-level routines for resolution. A useful tool for protection against error conditions is the `try catch` construct:

```
try
    thisSample = data(iSample);
catch IndexError
    index = min(iSample, nSamples);
    thisSample = data(index);
end
```

Another line of defense is to use properly ordered expressions in `if` statements so that evaluation short circuiting can avoid evaluation of expressions that will trigger an error:

```
if exist('a') && ~isempty(a)
   :
end
```

263. Make Error Messages Informative

Where possible, supplement the MATLAB warning or error message with specific information that will help the user understand the issue and what to do about it. Write proscriptive error messages. It is more useful to tell a user what to do about an error than to simply state that an error has occurred.

Replace

```
error('Argument error')
```

with

```
error('Make beta between 0 and 1.')
```

264. Use Message IDs with Errors and Warnings

Message IDs provide additional useful information and allow selective disabling.

Replace

```
error('Make beta between 0 and 1.')
```

with

```
error('foo: parameter check','Make beta
between 0 and 1.')
```

265. Use Exceptions

An exception object supports more flexibility in dealing with an error condition than a simple error function. Provide an exception argument for the `catch` command in a `try catch` construct that works with errors.

266. Support Error Returns

The best practice is to use exception handling for function errors. This makes it easier to handle the error at the most appropriate level. If you choose not to use exceptions, you can use function error return codes. If the return code is numerical, then it should be integer. By convention, the number 1 or a positive integer should be used for the absence of an error. Zero or a negative number should be used for an error condition. It is good practice to also return a message on error.

Do not use the implicit error return of a function in `if` or `switch` constructs. This practice is more difficult to understand, and it removes the opportunity to grab the error message.

Replace

```
if foo(in)<=0
    % Deal with error.
end
```

with

```
[errorCode, errorMessage] = foo(in);
if errorCode
    % Deal with error.
end
```

267. Use Appropriate Assertions.

In MATLAB, the `assert` function is closely related to `error`. It can act as a replacement for the basic `if error` sequence. For example

```
assert (x<=0)
```

is equivalent to

```
if x>0
    error
end
```

Assertions can also replace basic `try catch` constructs. A series of `assert` statements can be more compact than a series of `if error` or `try catch` constructs.

For some developers, assertion is used only for an "impossible" condition, whereas `error` is used for an unlikely and problematic condition. Others use assertion to uncover programming defects and `error` to catch data-related problems.

Output Style

268. Learn to Use `sprintf`

MATLAB provides the function `int2str` to produce a number with no decimal places and `num2str` to produce a number with up to four decimal places. You can achieve more flexibility in the number of decimal places with `sprintf` or `fprintf` as in

```
sprintf('%5.2f', value)
```

269. Learn to Use Tex

You can include Tex markup in character strings to include special characters and symbols in the resulting strings. This capability is especially useful to enhance labels and text entries for graphs.

Tests

We test to increase confidence in the code because untested software fails. Test to reduce defects, and test enough to reduce fear of defects. The process of writing and running tests can uncover design , structural, and logical problems. Responding to the tests can make the code more robust, readable, and well structured. Consider that any function too difficult to test well is probably too difficult to write correctly.

Writing test code can be as difficult as writing production code because it must meet the same quality standards. Readability is essential in test code. In most cases, the guidelines for test code are the same as those for production code. There are a few differences in naming and organization that support usability.

270. Write at Least One Test for Every Function or Method

This practice will improve the quality of the initial version of the function and the reliability of changed versions. Thinking through and writing test code can help better define the functionality and arguments of the function. The test routine should verify response to the defined number and types of arguments. It should also test the envelope conditions.

Update tests when you change production code. Be sure that your test suite covers any change in behavior. In general, you should add rather than delete tests.

271. Write Small Tests

Thorough testing requires a set of focused tests. You will find it easier to evaluate the output of a small test than a long complicated one and to trace any test failure back to relevant code.

Do not write tests within production code files. Writing a test in its own file is better than using an embedded test subfunction. The test is more likely to be complete, and the production code is less likely to depend on the test code.

It is also awkward to use a test subfunction for automated testing.

272. Write Uncoupled Tests

Write the test code so that the results do not depend on the order of testing. Test code will change, and interdependent tests will cause even more debugging. In general, each section of test code should include its own setup, evaluation, and cleanup.

273. Write Tests with Boolean Outputs

You can best automate testing, especially when running multiple tests, by writing tests to have Boolean outputs. Typically, the output value is true if everything works or false when at least one case fails. Code passes the tests if any valid input produces the correct output and if any invalid input is detected and coped with.

274. Test for Expected Exceptions

Your production code may include exception statements. Your test code should trigger the exception, catch the exception, and make sure it is the expected one. An example would be a function that generates an exception for invalid input. The test code would call the function with an invalid input variable. The function fails this test if the exception is not generated.

275. Write Tests You Can Automate

Support test automation by using a program or framework that runs the tests. In general, write one test function or class that includes all unit tests for each production function or class unless it becomes too long. If it is too long, then break it up by type of test, feature, or method.

Consider writing unit tests that do not stop on error. Getting results from multiple unit tests can help determine what went wrong.

276. Use Related Names in the Function and the Test Code

Using the same or related variable names in both places makes it easier to scan the test and production code for variable-to-argument matching or naming issues. When calling the function

```
function foo(alpha, beta)
```

use

```
foo(alpha, beta)
```

or

```
foo(thisAlpha, thisBeta)
```

277. Identify Test Files by Name

Use the word `test` as a prefix in the test file name to support easy file organization. Using a distinctive name style for test functions and files makes it easier to select test code for automation and to prevent production code from depending on test code. Using a test name that is closely related to the function name makes it easier to find the appropriate test code. For example, use the name

```
test_foo
```

with the function foo.

278. Develop Test Patterns

In general, the test code should require less time to develop than the code to be tested. Yet, test code is as difficult to write correctly as project code. The strategy is to develop test code patterns. The patterns could, for example, produce interesting inputs or evaluate expected outputs. When the inputs are common to multiple tests, write setup code to produce them.

Thorough testing may require writing tests that go beyond obvious user stories or stated requirements. Patterns can help define these important but underspecified tests. Your test patterns might include looking for problems with boundary data such as extreme values and empty variables.

279. Consider Tests for External Software

You may want to write tests for external software that interfaces with your own to be sure that you understand how it works. You can also run these tests when new versions of the external software are released to catch any problematic changes.

Data Files

280. Make Use of mat Files

Consider storing preprocessed input data in a mat file for multiple processing accesses. Organize data into arrays, structures, or objects with meaningful names. Organize the data so that access and computation are as straightforward as possible. Mat files have a big advantage over other file types in that they maintain the variable names associated with the data.

281. Follow Database Conventions

Use standard database arrangements for data arrays. In the usual database organization for a data table, each column is a field, parameter, or variable. Each row is a record, sample, or observation.

Good database practices include selection criteria (and having a good field for selection), consistency (names and types), sorting (and having a good field for sorting), and input validation (checking before storing).

282. Follow the MATLAB Convention for Data Array Orientation

Put time series in columns of data arrays. This is the default orientation for most MATLAB functions. Similarly, arrange data that will be summarized and compared so that the summary is along columns and the comparison is along rows. For example, consider a data array of temperatures by date for several cities. The data for each city would be a column, and the data for each date would be a row. For associated variables, the dates would be in a column vector, and the city names would be in a row cell array.

Programming Summary

Write code and refine it to meet high standards. Write readable code that is easy to use, modify, and test. Your users will thank you, and your life will be better.

Use variables consistently. Avoid confusing definition or redefinition. Make the meaning of constants clear. Minimize the use of global constants and variables.

Write short, easy-to-read expressions and statements. Use intermediate variables to capture the meaning of expressions. Use spaces, parentheses, and the order of variables and operators to clarify expressions.

Write loops simply so that they are easy to read and get correct. Be careful of starting and ending details. Initialize computed variables to avoid surprises and achieve better performance.

Write `if` and `switch` constructs simply so that they are easy to read and get correct. Simplify selection expressions, but avoid redundant selections. Extract code from selection blocks to subfunctions if that clarifies the construct. In general, include `else` or `otherwise`.

Write most procedural code as simple, modular functions. Avoid unnecessary interaction or duplication between functions. Provide clear and expected input and output arguments. Minimize the number of input arguments, but give them reasonable flexibility.

Write object-oriented code in small cohesive classes. Try to keep classdef files short and well organized. Do not make properties public unless you need to. Write easy-to-use public methods. Follow established conventions for constructor and overload methods.

6.

Files and Organization

The organization of code and data files in directories can have a significant impact on ease of use. Separate project-specific and general-purpose m-files to make them easier to use and to integrate with the MATLAB product.

Toolboxes

284. Organize General-Purpose m-Files in Toolboxes

Develop general-purpose program libraries or toolboxes to increase productivity. A library is particularly helpful for related functions, such as statistics or time series analysis, that are useful in more than one application domain.

Write your toolboxes for sharing. Standards are higher for public toolboxes that you share with others than for personal toolboxes for your own use. Improve the quality of your code by having others use and criticize it. A public toolbox should be usable by nonexperts and customizable and extensible by experts.

285. Put Test Files in a Separate Directory

In general, do not release test files in a production code toolbox directory. Putting the test files in their own directory makes the release separation easier. Using separate directories helps avoid any dependence of the production code on the test code.

286. Consider Writing Demo Files

Demo files provide the user with quick examples of the capabilities and uses of the functions in a toolbox. Demos often use graphical user interfaces (GUIs) or are graphics based, and they allow the user to see results without extensive programming.

Some users find it easier to learn how to work with a function or class by studying examples rather than syntax descriptions. Demo files provide an opportunity to show extended examples that would not fit in the comment-based documentation of a code module. The demo file directory is also a good place for published documentation files.

287. Use a Consistent Toolbox Folder Organization

Toolboxes from The MathWorks follow varying folder organizations. The most recent approach seems to be that a toolbox for audio processing would be in a directory named something like *audio* with subdirectories *audio*, *audiodemos*, and *audiogui*.

The *audiodemo* subdirectory contains demo scripts, data files, a demo.xml file, possibly private subdirectories, and an HTML subdirectory for published results. The demo.xml file supports integration with the Help system. The *audio* subdirectory contains the toolbox m-files, a Contents m-file, an info.xml file, and possibly some private subdirectories. The info.xml file supports integration with the Help system.

Naming the m-file subdirectory the same as the toolbox directory (*audio*) is confusing; it is better to use a different name such as *functions*, *programs*, or *tools*.

288. Provide for Integration with MATLAB

Add the toolbox locations to the MATLAB path so that they are easy to use. Also add the function, demo, and GUI subdirectories to the MATLAB path. Pay attention to the order of directories on the path to avoid surprises caused by function name shadowing.

289. Provide a Reference Page for Every Public Function

Use the Publish feature to produce documentation of the function from its m-file. Having the reference information source and the code in the same file makes it easier to keep the two consistent. Make your HTML reference page look like the standard reference pages in the Help browser.

290. Integrate the Reference Pages with the Help Browser

Build a search database for your reference pages. Put an info.xml file that points to your reference pages in the toolbox function folder so that it is on the MATLAB path. Even simple functions benefit from search access through the Help browser.

291. Do not Make Your Toolbox a Subfolder of the MATLAB Folder

The MathWorks recommends that you do not make your toolbox a subfolder of the MATLAB folder. This will help avoid problems when you add to your MATLAB installation or install a new release.

This also means that you should put your toolbox reference or Help folder under your toolbox folder rather than under the MATLAB Help folder.

Project Files

292. Organize Your Project-Specific Files by Project Directory

In general, avoid using the default MATLAB work directory for anything except temporary work. This directory may be lost and will be off the default path when the MATLAB product is upgraded.

293. *Organize Your Data Directory for Ease of Access*

A data file will usually be written only once, but it may be read multiple times. Group data files and organize them in directories so that they are easy to find and read automatically.

For projects with small amounts of data, it can be convenient to place data and MATLAB m-files in a single directory. For example, the directory

```
analyze_gear
```

might contain

```
foo.m
blatz.m
wheel.mat
strut.mat
```

For projects with large amounts of data, use program and data subdirectories to simplify directory listings and ease backup policies. For example, the directory

```
analyze_gear
```

might contain the subdirectory

```
programs
```

containing

```
foo.m
blatz.m
```

and the subdirectory

```
data
```

containing

```
wheel_101.mat
wheel_102.mat
```

```
strut_101.mat
strut_102.mat
```

For projects with very large amounts of data, use multiple data subdirectories. In addition to easing backup, this organization also supports simple automated data file access. For example, the directory

```
analyze_gear
```

might contain the subdirectory

```
programs
```

containing

```
foo.m
blatz.m
```

and the subdirectory

```
data
```

containing subdirectories

```
plane_101
plane_102
```

each containing

```
wheel.mat
strut.mat
```

Organization Summary

Organize your code and data files in directories in a way that supports easy use and development. It is usually best to avoid placing your code in the standard MATLAB tree or in the default MATLAB working directory.

Use separate directories for each project and for your general-purpose files. Put your production m-files and their test files in separate directories. Put your production m-files and their reference page files in separate directories. Integrate your reference pages with the Help browser.

7.

Development

MATLAB now has the capability for serious projects, not just casual prototyping. As projects get bigger and team size grows, explicit and consistent development practices become more important. MATLAB is used with a range of recognized development practices from traditional to more recent agile approaches. This chapter presents techniques and strategies that are generally applicable to most of these practices. It also includes some items that are agile-specific.

Traditional approaches tend to have formal documented specifications and detailed design up front, with code documentation and testing near the end of the process. Agile approaches promote writing code and tests early, refactoring often to produce design, and placing less emphasis on formal documentation.

The goal of any development is software that works, usually including properties such as stability, correctness, extensibility, and maintainability. All serious development approaches include elements such as design, documentation, and test. The project deliverables are code (main and test) and documentation (of software, process, and evaluation).

Most software projects are constrained by developer time. Use practices that make the best use of your limited time and are effective in your work environment. Despite schedule pressures, make time to learn about important elements of the language, features of the development environment, and best practices.

Design

Software design should start with two deceptively simple questions. What is the purpose of the software? Who will be the users? The purpose of a software project is usually to provide benefits to users. These benefits should be expressible as features. A major part of software design is decomposing these features into functionality. The users may be other software developers, but more often they are people with less software knowledge. The priority for most users is a trouble-free means to use the code rather than a long list of features.

294. Expect Change

Requirements are often incomplete and can change with little warning. Usage changes. Technical software, perhaps more than other types, will be used for new and different tasks. Expect changes.

You can plan for change by writing code to a consistent style and maintaining a thorough test suite. You can also adapt to incomplete and changing requirements by providing early prototypes to the users.

295. Include Appropriate Flexibility

Too little flexibility in your code can lead to a lot of work in the future. Too much can lead to a lot of work now. Your experience will guide you toward the right amount of flexibility.

Code that will be part of a toolbox or shared with others should typically be more flexible than code with a short lifetime and for your own use. The `inputParser` object is a good example of flexible code. It is used by many people to work in many different functions. The inputParser only does two things, but it is flexible enough to work with a variety of input argument lists.

296. Use the Right Algorithm

Scalability and fast performance come not so much from code optimization as from design and selection of the right algorithm. Appropriate algorithms and even tested code are available for many tasks. Do not waste time coding the wrong algorithm.

297. Program by Contract

Design module interfaces to pre and post conditions to support thoughtful development and verification. When modifying code, try to extend it (maintain interfaces and functionality) rather than making a change that can cause problems with other routines.

298. Write for Automation

Avoid `keyboard`, `input`, and `pause` commands when possible. Use a parameter file instead. This approach is particularly important for automated test and data analysis.

299. Make Associated Data Easy to Use

Carefully consider what data belong together based on what will be done with them. Often the organization of the data will indicate the best way to organize the code. Typically, data that go together should be placed in a structure or object. A structure can be better than an object if the object would be only a data container that has no behavior.

300. Recompute When Data Changes

When input data changes, try to recompute all results rather than doing a partial update. This practice will help reduce inconsistencies in dependent variable values. If the data and the results are in a single object or a structure, any method or function that changes the data should probably recompute the results.

301. Leave Code Optimization for Last or Never

Optimization for speed or memory usage tends to make code more cryptic and may not be needed. Also, defining the optimization technique, implementing it, and testing it all take development time.

302. Consider Coding Standards

Coding standards specify common elements for the code that make it easier to share and use code and easier to understand the ideas expressed in the code. They are programming rules that reduce the likelihood of introducing errors into the programs. They go beyond style guidelines to address topics such as use and behavior. Examples include specific variable names, input and output formats, and processing algorithms.

Use of coding standards can

- Increase product reliability, code portability, ease of maintenance, and usage lifetime.
- Increase programmer productivity through reducing the learning curve for a language.
- Increase team productivity by facilitating communication.
- Reduce development and support costs.
- Streamline code reviews.
- Increase the ease with which certification is obtained.

Development Practices

Modern development approaches rely on incremental iteration for most projects. Because MATLAB is largely an interpreted language, it is very appropriate for this type of approach. Using the MATLAB integrated development environment tools with consistent code refinement will ease the development of quality code.

303. Develop in Small Steps

Build confidence in the code incrementally. It is more likely that you can write a few lines of code at a time without error than many lines. Finding the bug in a few lines of code is much easier than finding it in a large number of lines.

Automate as many development steps as you can. Change code in small steps and test it promptly, particularly when refactoring. Check code into version control early and often.

304. Develop in the Editor

Write code in the Editor rather than in the Command Window. It will likely be better structured, have better style, and still be easy to execute incrementally during development.

305. Use Version Control

Version control is the best way to manage and document code changes. It is helpful for solo development and almost essential for team development. Use a version control application that is appropriate for your development environment. MATLAB currently supports direct integration with only a few source control applications. You may need to find a third-party interface or use a manual process.

306. Run Tests Often

Test the production code that you write as you write it. This testing is the first instance of use of the code. It provides quick feedback on code quality and the effect of changes. Automate all testing as much as possible so that it is easy and quick to run.

307. Run all Tests Before Release

Code that is tested only in development environments may fail after release. Run all tests in a prerelease environment to be sure that the code in the release is complete, consistent, and runs correctly in the target environment.

MATLAB IDE Tools

Use the MATLAB integrated development environment features. These tools can improve code, enforce consistency, and shorten development time.

308. Try the MATLAB Editor

The MATLAB Editor has many features that will help you apply these guidelines and write better code. It provides color syntax highlighting, selective code execution, automatic indentation, and parenthesis matching. The M-Lint feature helps improve code quality by providing prompt feedback on errors and questionable usage. The Editor includes debugging features for efficient trouble shooting. In addition to selective code execution, the cell feature also helps clarify blocks of code and support publishing.

Most developers will use the MATLAB Editor. If you prefer a different editor, use one that at least supports color coding, automated indenting, selective execution, and search and replace. You will probably open the code in the MATLAB Editor at some point to use its additional features. Set your editor preferences so that the code looks the same in both editors.

309. Use Smart Indent

The Editor automatically provides indentation for loops and selection constructs while you type. If you write code statements out of order because of insertion or modification, then they can lack proper indentation. The Smart Indent feature can quickly adjust code layout to provide consistent indenting.

310. Use Find and Replace

If you change a variable name, then use the editor Find and Replace feature. Do not expect that you will always be successful in making changes by just scanning the code. It is difficult to manually find all instances of the old name and spell the new name correctly. Similarly, you can use the Search Across Files feature to find occurrences of a name to change in multiple files.

311. Pay Attention to M-Lint

The MATLAB product does not include a code checking tool that *enforces* coding or style standards. It does provide M-Lint, an Editor tool that is primarily intended to point out coding errors. M-Lint also provides some warning messages that relate to style standards and best practices.

Heed the M-Lint error and warning messages as you write. Catch errors and poor usage quickly, and improve the code. Some of the warning messages can actually reveal errors. The message

```
The value assigned here to variable 'readOne'
might be unused.
```

can be caused by an inconsistently spelled variable name.

312. Use Consistent Preference Settings

Establish standard editor settings for tab and indent size, right-hand text limit line, and comment formatting. If you develop in a group, then try to agree on these settings so that you can more easily scan each other's code.

313. Use the Debugger Effectively

Many users new to MATLAB or to debugging rely on basic practices such as semicolon removal, or simple functions such as `display` or `fprintf`. This strategy can be effective, but using the Debugger is often more efficient.

You should change one of the default Debugger settings to make better use of the Editor integration. Turn on "Always stop if error" when debugging functions. With this menu selection, the Editor opens the file when an error occurs and puts a cursor close to the problem site.

There are two features of Debugger operation that may be unexpected. It stacks up debug conditions so you may have to exit the debug mode or continue several times to return to the non-debug mode. Also the "Exit debug" menu selection or command sometimes turns off the "Always stop if error" setting.

314. Use the TODO/FIXME Report

When you cannot resolve an issue as you write, insert TODO or FIXME comments. These comments are gathered by the TODO/FIXME Directory Report, which makes it easy to find the files and areas that you have identified for rework. Most developers do not make a distinction between TODO and FIXME. They simply use TODO. Make the format of these comments consistent across a project, for example:

```
% TODO : Revise if fraction is changed to percent.
```

315. Use the Profiler

Do not rewrite code just for speed unless you have to. If you do need faster execution, then be sure that you are changing the code that will make the most difference. The slow parts of your code may not be where you expect. Use the Profiler to find bottlenecks in execution speed and, in some cases, suggestions for speed improvement. You can also use the Profiler to assess test coverage of code lines.

316. Use the Dependency Report

When assembling a toolbox or preparing for release, run the Dependency Report to verify that required child functions are included. This report can also reveal any unintended dependencies of one function on others, especially dependence on functions that you do not intend to release.

317. Publish During Development

Use the Publish feature to view comments in a form that is more readable than plain text in the Editor window. This will make it easier to keep the code and comments consistent. It will also help you determine the right format for header comments and for comments within the code body.

318. Find a Desktop Layout That Works for You

Reduce the distraction of window focus changes by arranging your most used windows in the MATLAB desktop. Many programmers find that the most useful desktop includes the Editor, the Command Window, the Workspace browser, and the Current Folder window. If you write code in the Editor and use version control, the Command History window is not important enough for the screen space that it would require.

Development Summary

Consciously use a development approach to produce better software in less time. There are several approaches in use, and you can define your own hybrid. These approaches share several common elements when used with MATLAB.

Write well-designed small modules – functions, methods, and classes. Each module should do one thing or only a few things. Simple code is better than complicated code. A module that is simple but flexible in the inputs it accepts is better than one that is too ambitious in its number or variety of outputs.

When relevant well-written code already exists, use it as a starting point for your own.

Use the tools in the MATLAB integrated development environment to increase code quality and save you time. Especially useful elements of the IDE include the Desktop, the Editor, M-Lint, the Debugger, the TODO/FIXME report, the Profiler, and the Publish feature.

Develop in the MATLAB Editor or one with equivalent capability. Use the Editor features to make it easy to write code with clear layout and consistent identifier naming.

Use M-Lint to find and fix errors, poor usage, and poor style. Use the Publish feature to improve commenting and help keep comments consistent with the code.

Write thorough test functions as you write the project code. Write the test code so that you can run it automatically during development and before release.

Keywords

Avoid using MATLAB keywords for variable, function, or file names. These keywords may be version dependent, and you can produce a current list using the iskeyword command:

```
iskeyword
ans =
        'break'
        'case'
        'catch'
        'classdef'
        'continue'
        'else'
        'elseif'
        'end'
        'for'
        'function'
        'global'
        'if'
        'otherwise'
        'parfor'
        'persistent'
        'return'
        'spmd'
        'switch'
        'try'
        'while'
```

is* function list

Avoid using MATLAB is* function names for variable, function or file names. A recent list of these function names is

is*	isinf	ispc
isa	isinteger	ispref
isappdata	isinterface	isprime
iscell	isjava	isprop
iscellstr	isKey	isreal
ischar	iskeyword	isscalar
iscom	isletter	issorted
isdir	islogical	isspace
isempty	ismac	issparse
isequal	ismember	isstr
isevent	ismethod	isstrprop
isfield	isnan	isstruct
isfinite	isnumeric	isstudent
isfloat	isobject	isunix
isglobal	isocaps	isvalid
ishandle	isocolors	isvarname
ishold	isonormals	isvector

Glossary

accessor
A method that gets the value of a property.

argument
Functions have zero or more input arguments and zero or more output arguments. The input arguments are the best way to supply data and parameters to the function. The output arguments are the best way to transfer results and related information from the function.

assertion
A statement that evaluates a logical expression.

Boolean
Boolean variables and expressions only have the values true or false.

camel case
An identifier is in camel case when the words in a compound name are joined without spaces. The first letter of each word within the compound name is capitalized. The first letter of the first word can be capitalized (UpperCamelCase) or not (lowerCamelCase).

CapWords
See UpperCamelCase.

class
A class is the formal definition of an object. It is like a template or blueprint that describes a set of objects with common characteristics.

cohesion

The degree to which class methods and properties or function statements belong together or relate to each other.

constructor

A method that initializes a new instance of a class.

coupling

The degree to which two or more functions or objects are dependent on each other.

Editor

A component of the MATLAB Integrated Development Environment that supports, debugging, publishing, code analysis, and selective execution of code, as well as the usual editing capabilities.

encapsulation

The degree to which the internal data and implementation of an object are hidden from external access.

fieldname

The name of a field of a structure.

global

A global constant or variable is one that is declared with the global keyword so that it becomes available in all workspaces.

handle

A reference to an object that is derived from the handle superclass. A function handle is a value that can be used to call a function indirectly.

Help Report

A feature in the MATLAB development environment that lists discrepancies between function header comments and recommended practice.

Hungarian notation

A naming convention that includes type in variable names. It has proven to be more trouble than it is worth in most contexts.

identifier
Identifiers are the words used when writing programs (e.g., variable names, function names, object names, reserved words).

import
Add a package or class to the current workspace.

inheritance
The mechanism that provides more specialized classes with the characteristics of more general classes.

inputParser
An object that is used to parse and validate function input arguments.

InterCap
See UpperCamelCase.

interface
For classes, an interface is an example of an abstract class that defines the interaction of an object with the external code. For functions, the interface consists of the input and output arguments.

iterator
An index of a for or while loop.

JIT
MATLAB provides Just-In-Time compilation of some sections of code to improve performance.

keyword
A word that is reserved in the MATLAB language for special usage.

lowerCamelCase
An identifier is in lowerCamelCase when the words in a compound name are joined without spaces, the first letter of each word within the compound name is capitalized, and the first letter of the first word is not capitalized.

maintenance
  Modifying code to fix problems or extend capability.

mixedCase
  See lowerCamelCase.

object
  A specific instance of a class. Objects encapsulate data and operations in software with defined interfaces.

operator
  A function that performs computations on operands. Typically, the operator can be written in symbols or as a function name. The operands are typically one or two variables, expressions, or objects.

parameter
  A variable, typically within a context such as a parameter-value pair.

ProperCase
  See UpperCamelCase.

Publish
  A feature in the MATLAB development environment that supports producing nicely formatted documents from scripts and functions.

refactor
  Refactoring code is the process of changing its internal structure for better design or style without changing its external behavior or functionality. It is a disciplined way to clean up code.

scope
  The scope of a variable refers to the number of workspaces in which it is used or the number of lines of code its use spans. A variable with global scope is used in more than one workspace. A variable with local scope is used within a single workspace and typically within one block of code.

shadowing

    A function is shadowed if a variable or other function within its scope has the same name. This makes the shadowed function inaccessible and can lead to undesirable consequences.

side effects

    Things that a function does other than provide values for its output arguments.

Smart Indent

    A feature of the Editor that can produce standard indenting in a selected sequence of statements.

Title_Case

    A "belt and suspenders" approach to identifier naming that uses capital letters to begin all words in a compound name and has an underscore between words. Use of Title_Case is not common.

toolbox

    A collection of functions with related use. Relationships might include application area, such as image processing; theme, such as smoothing; or project, such as stability control.

unit test

    Code written to test one module or "unit" of code, typically a function, object, or method. A unit test does three things: it builds the required data, calls the target to process the data, and checks the result.

UpperCamelCase

    An identifier is in UpperCamelCase when the words in a compound name are joined without spaces, the first letter of each word within the compound name is capitalized, and the first letter of the first word is capitalized. Typically, UpperCamelCase is used for class and object names.

Bibliography

Attaway, Stormy. *MATLAB: A Practical Introduction*. (Boston: Elsevier, 2009)

Baldwin, Kenneth et al. *The Elements of C# Style*. (New York: Cambridge University Press, 2006)

Beck, Kent. *Test-Driven Development*. (Boston: Addison-Wesley, 2003)

Crispin, Lisa and Tip House. *Testing Extreme Programming*. (Boston: Addison-Wesley, 2003)

Fowler, Martin et al. *Refactoring: Improving the Design of Existing Code*. (Boston: Addison-Wesley, 1999)

Geotechnical Software Services. "Java Programming Style Guidelines, Version 6.1." (2008) Available at: http://geosoft.no/development/javastyle.html (accessed August 2, 2010)

Hoff, Todd. "C++ Coding Standard." (2008) Available at: www.possibility.com/Cpp/CppCodingStandard.html (accessed August 2, 2010)

Hunt, Andrew and David Thomas. *The Pragmatic Programmer*. (Boston: Addison-Wesley, 1999)

Johnson, Richard. "MATLAB Programming Style Guidelines, Version 1.5." (2002) Available at: http://datatool.com/downloads/matlab_style_guidelines.pdf (accessed August 2, 2010)

Kernighan, Brian and Rob Pike. *The Practice of Programming*. (Indianapolis: Addison-Wesley, 1999)

Kernigan, Brian and P J Plauger. *The Elements of Programming Style* (New York: McGraw-Hill, 1988)

Martin, Robert. *Clean Code.* (New York: Prentice Hall, 2008)

McConnell, Steve. *Code Complete.* (Redmond, WA: Microsoft Press, 2004)

Misfeldt, Trevor. *The Elements of C++ Style.* (New York: Cambridge University Press, 2004)

Oliveira, Suely and David Stewart. *Writing Scientific Software.* (New York: Cambridge University Press, 2006)

Sun Microsystems. Java Code Conventions. (Palo Alto, CA: Sun Microsystems, 1999)

van Rossum, Guido and Barry Warsaw. "Style Guide for Python Code." (2001) Available at: www.python.org/dev/peps/pep-0008/ (accessed August 2, 2010)

Vermeulen, Allan et al. *The Elements of Java Style.* (New York: Cambridge University Press, 2000)

Wikipedia. "Programming Style." (July 1, 2010) Available at: http://en.wikipedia.org/wiki/Programming_style (accessed August 2, 2010)

Index